MASTERING
TRANSITIONS

MASTERING
TRANSITIONS

Ed Bratcher
Robert Kemper
Douglas Scott

MULTNOMAH

Portland, Oregon 97266

MASTERING TRANSITIONS
© 1991 by Christianity Today, Inc.
Published by Multnomah Press
Portland, Oregon 97266

Multnomah Press is a ministry of Multnomah School of the Bible, 8435 N.E. Glisan Street, Portland, Oregon 97220.

Printed in the United States of America.

Library of Congress Cataloging-in-Publication Data

Bratcher, Edward B., 1924–
    Mastering transitions / Ed Bratcher, Robert Kemper, Douglas Scott.
       p. cm.
    ISBN 0-88070-372-5
    1. Clergy—Relocation I. Kemper, Robert G.   II. Scott, Douglas
III. Title.
BV664.B73   1991
253'.2—dc20   90-20214
                                        CIP

91 92 93 94 95 96 97 98 99 00 - 10 9 8 7 6 5 4 3 2 1

CONTENTS

Introduction

I grew up in the West — restless pioneer country. Large reclamation projects had spilled water into our desert valley several decades before my birth, and folks had moved there to make the land — and their transplanted lives — blossom.

My great-grandparents and grandparents — a warehouseman, a fruit grower, a teamster turned woodworker — joined the emigrant band. They arrived in the Yakima Valley in different decades, but they came for similar reasons: a relentless urge to better themselves, to get ahead, to find something that was missing.

The Land of the Leaving

My ancestors weren't atypical. There's something in the American stock, something we've gained through living on a continent you had to move to get to, something drawn from raw contact with a land with broad horizons — something that seems to keep many of us pulling up our roots and finding a new valley just over the next ridge.

For pastors, who remain circuit riders of sorts, that "moving experience" is a common one. We go away to college, and perhaps even further away to seminary (in more ways than one, some parishioners lament). And then upon graduation and ordination, we'll likely hang our diplomas and open our Bibles in an unfamiliar community.

How often my wife and I have driven through a town and marveled, "Who knows, we could live here someday!" Yet, although we could live most anywhere, as pastors we rarely choose the specific place. Unlike the barber fresh out of barber college, we normally can't just head back to our home town and set up shop. Somebody has to invite us — *call* us — wherever we go.

And doesn't it seem that God, surely exercising his rich sense of humor, has a habit of surprising us with his choices for our lives? Why else would a Colorado kid like my friend Dave be called to pastor in downstream, flatland Texas? And how else would I, this premiere geographical chauvinist for the Northwest, find myself landlocked on the Great Prairie, days from a decent glacier or rain forest?

Why? Because God has been moving his people around since Noah hit the seas, and Abraham, the trade routes. Because God had a transition in mind, he issued a call. And we restless, trying-to-improve-ourselves descendants of emigrants hit the trail for a new challenge.

Jesus said to his followers, "*Go*, therefore, and make disciples." Sometimes I wonder if we know when to quit going. For instance, in a given year, around 9 or 10 percent of Presbyterian pastors delight the "Adventures in Moving" industry.

Mastering Transitions

Chances are, then, you are either just getting over a transition, in the process of moving, or soon to be joining the band of peripatetic pastors. If that's the case, we want to help make your pastoral transition the best of experiences.

Mastering Transitions, book six in the practical Mastering Ministry series, is written with you in mind. We believe the chapters you are about to read can help smooth — and even polish! — your ministry move. Of course, we can't guarantee your transition will be simple, or painless, or even immediately successful. But as you read and adapt the counsel of your fellow-travelers, and most of all as you go in answer to God's call and with his hand upon you, we believe your move can be *good*.

The writers of this book on transitions were chosen by the editors of LEADERSHIP for their accumulated experience and insight into what might be called "the crisis of relocation."

Edward B. Bratcher

Edward Bratcher — Ed, to his congregation and friends — was a missionary kid, born during a Kentucky furlough but raised in Brazil. At 15 he completed high school in Brazil (speaking Portuguese) and before his nineteenth birthday had graduated from Baylor University.

While in the service (as a naval officer on submarine duty in World War II), Ed married, and after he was discharged in 1946, he headed for Southern Baptist Theological Seminary in Louisville.

He has served churches in Aurora, Indiana; West Point, Kentucky; Austin, Texas; Kansas City; and Waynesboro, Virginia, before retiring from Manassas (Virginia) Baptist Church in December 1989, after fifteen years of service there.

Along the way, Ed has earned a Ph.D. (from his seminary), taught biblical archaeology and Greek, and received a denominational grant to research the personal and professional needs of ministers. That grant resulted in, among other things, his book, *The Walk-on-Water Syndrome* (Word).

Since retirement, Ed and his wife, Marjorie, have lived in

Durham, North Carolina. Ed has almost mastered the use of his retirement gift — a computer he has named "Legion" — while also maintaining a schedule of writing, traveling, and speaking. The Bratchers have three children and two grandchildren.

Ed is a man of calm intensity. Liveliness and graciousness combine with wisdom and experience to produce a statesman who knows ministry — both the joy of serving God through the church, and the cares and burdens that attend pastoral tenure. He also knows his fellow pastors, and loves them, and wants to grant to them a measure of the hard-earned insights he has picked up through forty-two years of ministerial transitions.

Robert G. Kemper

When last I changed pastorates, Robert Kemper's *Beginning a New Pastorate* (Abingdon, 1978) was my road map. I found him to be an expert tour guide who knew the terrain. His perception comes from experience.

For Bob, experience came early, for he was born the son of a Congregational minister in Alton, Illinois. He received his undergraduate degree from Cornell College of Mt. Vernon, Iowa, and his theological education and degree come from the Federated Theological Faculty of the University of Chicago. In recognition of his accomplishments, the Chicago Theological Seminary later granted Bob a Doctor of Divinity degree.

Bob's experience includes three pastorates: one in Newton Falls, Ohio; another in Montclair, New Jersey; and his current position, at which he has served since 1973, at First Congregational Church (UCC) of Western Springs, Illinois, a Chicago suburb.

He has also been a Life Trustee and adjunct professor of preaching at Chicago Theological Seminary, a lecturer at the summer institute of Princeton Theological Seminary, and an instructor in church management at the Institute for Advanced Pastoral Studies.

From 1969 to 1973, he served as founding editor of *The Christian Ministry*, an international journal for parish clergy, and he was also an associate editor of *The Christian Century*. He writes a newsletter for clergy — *Colleague* — and has authored five books. One of his books, *An Elephant's Ballet,* is the autobiographical story of his struggle with an eye disease.

We first met with Bob in his church study, a comfortable chamber, pleasingly cluttered with books and mementos. Bob leads his 1,300-member congregation, serving as principal preacher and administrator of the multi-staff church, with the same deliberate and thoughtful approach that characterizes his writing.

Douglas G. Scott

Doug Scott was born and raised in Philadelphia, the city that nurtured the curious Ben Franklin. Perhaps that environment contributed to shaping Doug's active mind, which roams over a variety of subjects — from theology to bagpipes to spirituality.

This curiosity was molded by his education at Muskingum College in New Concord, Ohio, and at Philadelphia Divinity School (Episcopal), from where he graduated with honors in 1974. He then attended General Theological Seminary, New York City, which awarded him his S.T.M. degree.

After serving on the staff of Episcopal bishops in Pennsylvania and New York, be began parish work. He has served parishes in Tenafly and Hasbrouck Heights, New Jersey, and Smithtown, New York. Since 1984 he has been rector of Saint Martin's (Episcopal) Church in Radnor, Pennsylvania.

Along the way he has married, and his wife, Jane, has borne him three children. He's also managed to write a couple of books — one called *The Piobaireachd*, about bagpipes!

Doug's interests range wide because ultimately he sees God's hand in all of creation. Some people can meditate richly on things spiritual. Others can wax eloquent on the dynamics of a well-executed job interview. Doug Scott manages to do both, weaving the spiritual and temporal together in his ministry and writing, even when he's writing about transitions.

Let's Move On

Our moving crew, as you can see, brings a variety of experiences and viewpoints to this book. They come from the South, the

East, and the Midwest, as well as from three different denominations. Press them hard enough, and they'd probably admit to some disagreements among themselves. I'm sure each would at least tinker with some of the points the other two make.

But that's an added value in the Mastering Ministry books: a variety of insight from which to draw. We consider you gifted enough to take these chapters and transform them into some masterful transitions.

— James D. Berkley
contributing editor
LEADERSHIP Journal
Carol Stream, Illinois

PART ONE
Hearing a Call

Sometimes the church that seems the perfect fit doesn't want to try us on. And sometimes the church that seems wrong turns out to be ever so right. A call to a specific church can be as mysterious as a call to ministry.

— *Ed Bratcher*

CHAPTER ONE

Seeing God's Call in a Church's Call

After finishing two years of advanced research at Louisville Seminary, I was contacted by several churches, one of which particularly attracted me. So I sent my résumé, held conversations with the church, and talked with people who knew something about it. I anticipated eagerly the possibility of going there. But they didn't choose me as their pastor.

Eventually, a church in Manassas, Virginia, called me. At first, though, I wanted nothing to do with it. Marjie and I had seen the tremendous pressure on the lives of the many professionals in the community, and we said, "No way!" We'd never lived in a community like that. Add to that the lack of unity in the congregation, and I didn't think I could pastor effectively there.

But Marjie and I were part of a support group in Louisville at the time, and when we told them about the church in Manassas and all our reasons for turning it down, the group was unanimous: "As we see you and your gifts, we think you can minister there. We encourage you to consider going." So we did.

Sometimes the church that seems the perfect fit doesn't want to try us on. And sometimes the church that seems wrong turns out to be ever so right. A call to a specific church can be as mysterious as a call to ministry.

Although God's leading is difficult to determine in such matters, it's not impossible. When we consider prayerfully the following factors, I believe we can get a better handle on where God is calling us.

When Not to Leave

During my ministry, I found that when my own church was experiencing troubles, I was tempted to seek a new church. Eventually though, I realized I should wait until my church was doing well before I moved on.

Some people think I had it backwards. If everything is going well and ministry is fruitful, why leave? Conversely, if things are going downhill, isn't that a sign we are no longer effective and ought to move on?

Perhaps, but I decided never to leave a situation simply because I was facing difficulties. Consequently, in my ministry, and especially during conflict, I tried to remember the following guidelines:

● *Don't leave in the midst of major conflicts.* Naturally, there are always conflicts in a church. Pastors can't please everybody. But I felt any major conflicts should be worked through before a move is considered. Realistically, of course, this is not always possible, but I always felt I should try.

● *Don't leave because you're depressed.* Depression is a common problem among ministers, but it's a poor reason to leave a church. I decided if I were struggling with persistent or severe feelings of depression, I'd seek professional help before writing a resignation letter.

• *Don't leave just because you're being criticized.* When Martin Luther King, Jr., was assassinated, the ministers in our community decided to have a memorial service. Since our church had the largest sanctuary in town, I offered to hold the service there.

Some months later, at one of our congregational business meetings, a motion was made for my dismissal because I had failed to get proper permission from the buildings and grounds committee to hold the memorial service at our church. It was evident in the ensuing discussion that the real issue was my position on race relations, but the issue was raised as a question of procedure. The motion failed because, in fact, I had called the chairman of the buildings and grounds committee before the service and asked his advice.

But because the discussion of the motion was so heated, Marjie and I had some doubts. Later we went to a couple in the church and asked, "Do you think our time has ended here?" They told us to stick it out.

Several years later, we invited some deacons from other local churches to help serve Communion at a Maundy Thursday service. One of the deacons from our church was also our custodian, a black man, and no one offered any criticism. The congregation had reached a point where race relations were not the sore point they used to be.

So, I'm glad I didn't run when the first shot was fired.

• *Don't leave when the church is in deep debt.* I know a pastor who didn't want to face up to dealing with his church's indebtedness, so he headed off to another congregation — with devastating consequences for the church he left behind. So I consider the financial situation of the church I'm thinking of leaving before deciding to move on.

The second church I pastored was in the small Kentucky town of West Point, on the Ohio River. When my wife and I moved into the parsonage, which had been built in 1937 for five hundred dollars, we could see grass growing through cracks in the floor.

So the church borrowed five thousand dollars — a lot of money in 1950, especially for that church — to build a new parsonage. In addition, like many small churches, it had seen many pastors in its history, thirty-nine in fifty years. So it was difficult for them to make a financial commitment like that.

Three years later, when I had finished my Ph.D., I was ready to move on. But we still hadn't paid off the five thousand dollar loan for the parsonage. So I decided to stay for another year while we paid off the mortgage. Only then did I feel free to go.

● *Don't leave just because a larger church is interested in you.* This becomes a special temptation when we're facing difficulties in our church. Often our self-worth gets tied to our pastoral success, and our success is often tied to the size of our church.

However, I was able to curb my ambition, at least to some degree, by remembering a simple statistic: 80 percent of all churches have fewer than two hundred members. So I knew I had to be realistic: most pastors are not going to end up in a large church.

I also think of several young men I've known who went up the ladder of success too fast and just burned out. They never stayed anywhere long enough to mature and become the capable individuals they could be.

In addition, Jesus taught we have to be faithful in the little tasks before he can trust us with the big ones. One of those little tasks, I believed, was settling problems in one church before moving on.

Even if I was eventually to be called to a larger church, I didn't want to shortchange smaller churches along the way, by either leaving too soon or by treating them as mere way stations to a more important calling.

When Definitely to Leave

Nonetheless, there are many good reasons to seek a new call: to develop new ministry gifts, to change the focus of one's ministry, to move closer to extended family, to combine the pursuit of studies, among others. But there is one time when moving is not merely desirable but urgent.

My first pastorate was in a church near the town of Lawrenceburg, Indiana. The largest employer in Lawrenceburg was a distillery, and many of my parishioners worked there. Most of them were plumbers who attended to the pipes through which distillery liquids of all sorts run.

These people were personally against the use of alcohol but worked at the distillery because (a) if they didn't, somebody else would anyway, and (b) they were better able to provide for their families in the distillery than elsewhere in the community.

I had some reservations at the time I accepted the call. And after several months, I became extremely uncomfortable, because my salary was being paid, in essence, by the distillery. I made the difficult decision to resign, because I was afraid if I compromised what I believed to be right, I would soon start compromising myself in other areas.

In some cases then, the call to move may begin with the personal values God has planted in us. Each of us has issues about which we won't compromise. And if the community or church asks us to compromise, we know what to do.

Whatever the reason, when we've decided to seek a new call, a number of issues should be considered. The following were some of the most important to me.

People *and* Prayer

In seeking a specific call, I've often wondered how much to rely on human initiative and how much on God's initiative. I've been tempted by two extremes: to sell myself by playing politics or to become completely passive, thinking, *If God wants to call me to a particular church, he'll make sure it finds me.*

In the end, I've not been comfortable with either extreme. On the one hand, I think it's inappropriate to take a hard-sell approach to candidating. On the other hand, no pulpit committee ever received a telegram from God inscribed with the name of the person to be called; I've had to acknowledge that human beings play their part in the process.

In my mind, the ideal procedure works like this: I learn about a particular church and feel I understand some of its pressures and dynamics. I believe I am sensitive to the needs of the people and have gifts to help address those needs. So, either directly or through a friend, I present my résumé to the search committee, saying, "I believe I have the gifts and training to work in this situation, and I would like to work with you in seeking God's will."

I would discuss openly with the committee who I am and what gifts I have. In turn, I would encourage the committee to be open with me. There would be no manipulation or posturing. Together we would pray and seek divine guidance. That, to me, maintains the balance between the human and divine elements of a specific call.

Integrity Is the Best Policy

I've tried to follow a number of do's and don'ts in seeking a call, but all of them boil down to maintaining my integrity in the calling process.

● *In my résumé, don't blow achievements and credentials out of proportion.* I'm not a chaplain to a sports team because I led a couple of their Bible studies. I don't have an international ministry because I held a prayer meeting in a foreign country.

● *Don't use funds from my current church to make myself more marketable to a new church* — like taking out large advertisements in the local newspaper with my picture prominently displayed, or printing up a church brochure that emphasized my credentials.

● *Don't flood my friends with requests to be recommended to churches* without giving serious consideration to whether I could serve those churches effectively.

● *Be honest with myself and others.* Be honest about who I am. Be honest about my credentials and what they mean. Be honest about whether my gifts match the needs of a particular church. Be honest about what I feel God calling me to do.

Seeking a call to a church is a lot like dating. During courtship, we're tempted to avoid revealing ourselves completely to another for fear we might be rejected. Especially when we're strongly attracted to each other, we may never consider whether we're a good match.

Likewise, pastoral candidates and churches do a delicate little courtship dance. The candidates often hide their true identity and fail to consider honestly the prospective church's real situation. Sometimes we may deceive ourselves, thinking, *I wasn't able to handle that* (e.g., administration or calling) *in the past, but this situation will be different.*

At least during courtship, we have enough time to become honest with our loved one before we get married. In the calling of a pastor, things often happen quickly. So it's vital to be honest from the beginning.

What's Your Present Agenda?

When considering a call, we naturally consider what we want to do in a church. Sometimes we assume that we want to do what we've done well, using our gifts and expertise. But in my ministry, my interests often shifted. So part of the process of deciding a call involved deciding what I wanted to do in that call.

When I pastored churches in Austin, Texas, and Kansas City, I enjoyed working with building committees and constructing new sanctuaries. But by the time I went to Waynesboro, Virginia, I was ready to concentrate on preaching.

In Austin, Kansas City, and Waynesboro I actively advocated integration and acceptance of blacks. Later, although I remained committed to the same ideals, I no longer devoted such a large part of my time to race relations. That's one reason I finally turned down a church in Virginia that contacted me about serving as their pastor.

The church was located in a silk-stocking district that had succumbed to urban decay; most members of the congregation had moved to the suburbs. In addition, a significant black Baptist church was located just three blocks away.

When I spoke to the pulpit committee, I asked how much contact they had with this black church and how open they were to working with it to minister to the neighborhood. They said they weren't at all interested.

It was clear their views on working with the black church didn't mesh with mine. Furthermore, I didn't feel called to continue advocating integration and racial harmony with the same intensity. Seeing this was what was needed there, I decided it would be wrong for me to serve as their pastor.

All in the Family

I once received a call from a woman whose husband had just accepted a position that involved relocation. She was devastated. Her husband was convinced it was God's call, but she was totally unprepared for it. She wanted to support her husband but didn't think she could. They were at an impasse.

This is an easy trap to fall into. It was for me, anyway, particularly when the children were small.

Even though our whole family had been happy at our church in Austin, when I received an invitation from the Kansas City church, I was sure it was the place to go. But once we arrived, I realized my family was having trouble with the change. The people weren't as open and cordial as they had been in the Southwest, our children disliked the school system, and my wife had the added pressure of caring for my mother, who since our move had come to live with us.

Realizing my responsibilities as a Christian husband and father, I talked to my brothers about making other arrangements for my mother and opened myself to the possibility of another call.

After that, as I considered any move, I tried to ask myself questions like these: *Can my spouse be happy in this church or community? How will a move — or stay — affect our children? Will I be able to support my family adequately — emotionally and financially?* And of course, these questions require a lot of discussion not only with one's spouse but with the children as well.

Consider the Joy

I think it's legitimate to consider how much enjoyment and

fulfillment we are likely to find in a particular church. When the Manassas pulpit committee interviewed me, I told them I was considering writing a book on pastor-church relations and wanted to be able to participate in related conferences and seminars. When I asked if they would be comfortable with this, they said yes. If they had said no, I may not have accepted that call. Researching and writing that book was something I eagerly looked forward to.

As it turned out, I couldn't have finished that book without the encouragement of the deacons of that church. One deacon in particular would often ask, "How much writing have you done lately?" When I would explain that I had been busy with this and that, she would say, "Those other things will still be there. You're supposed to be writing."

So I'm glad I had an agreement with that church not only about my pastoral duties but also about activities that would bring me joy.

Social Setting Makes a Difference

I knew a capable pastor who left an established church in a county seat in Arkansas for a church in Austin. He had a newspaper column in Arkansas and was well recognized throughout the state. But when he got to Austin, he was a small fish in a big pond. And having become accustomed to pastoring an established church that moved along gently, he now had to think about the needs of a new and growing congregation. It was such a drastic change, he was never able to adjust.

I also knew a pastor who had moved from a church in a blue-collar community, where he had been highly effective, to a congregation of high-powered professionals. The pressures and needs of the people in his new church were substantially different and he didn't know how to communicate with them. He was a gifted pastor, but he just wasn't cut out for that kind of congregation.

Consequently, when it was time for me to consider a new call, I thought deeply about the type of setting in which I could thrive, and especially about those in which I couldn't.

God's Call in Retrospect

These are just some of the factors to consider in deciding a call, and I've not even touched on financial packages and congregational history and a dozen other aspects. But after we sift through these many, many questions, we then have to determine God's call as best we can. I say that because often we must decide on faith and can only see God's hand clearly in retrospect.

When it gets down to it, we're in the same situation as Abraham. Hebrews says he went out not knowing where he was going. And that's often true for us: we know we're called, we try to discern the call as best we can, but often we don't know where we're going. More often than not, it's only later that we see God's agenda.

In the meantime, even though we see through a glass darkly, we are called to persist in looking for the beckoning of God's hand.

An interview will determine whether this is God's call only when it reveals the real story, when through it we discover the heart of the congregation's expectations and hopes.

— Doug Scott

CHAPTER TWO

Getting the Real Story: A Guide to Candidating

I took a deep breath to push the fatigue from my mind and body. After traveling seven hours to be there, my wife and I were now holding cups of strong coffee, surrounded by thirty people, and trying to connect names with faces.

They examined us closely, some smiling, some sizing us up like wary customers looking for a used car. Four months of correspondence, telephone conversations, research, and prayer had brought us to that moment. Every facet of my life would soon be explored publicly. I knew I would need the endurance of a distance runner just to withstand this evening. I was being interviewed.

The church, a major congregation in the South, was looking for a senior pastor. They had sent me a bulky package of materials — results of a congregational self-study, membership statistics, a statement of mission and purpose, and comprehensive financial reports for the previous five years.

I, in turn, had provided them with my background and experience.

We had planned our three-day interview trip with surgical precision — the children were with my parents in Philadelphia, the dog was housed at a kennel, the airline connections were engineered so my absence would not be missed, and other clergy were covering for me. It had been expensive and exhausting, but we were excited about the possibilities.

As we moved to our chairs, front and center, I prayed for discernment, knowing our conversations the next three days might well affect the rest of our lives. The chairman stood to begin the discussion.

Looking at me over the tops of his reading glasses, he said, "Before we begin, I want y'all to know I had to live up with the Yankees for a year back in 1965, and I didn't like it one bit! What makes you think you're gonna be happy livin' down here?"

My wife and I exchanged glances and knew at once — it was all over.

That interview, at least, left no doubt about the congregation's attitudes. That's better than search committees and candidates performing a verbal dance trying to appear as attractive as possible in the ecclesiastical mating ritual. Often discussion is merely an exchange of theological pleasantries, with the tragic result that congregation and pastor don't really get to know each other. At best, this means the first year is spent discovering the truth. At worst, such a flawed process makes everyone disillusioned when unexpected attitudes, ideas, and commitments surface only after the pastor arrives.

How can candidates improve the situation? Can the interview itself be a constructive and even enjoyable process?

Yes. Approached carefully, the interview is an effective tool for discerning the congregation's expectations. The committee may not have thought back further than the former pastor's resignation, and their forward vision may be limited to moving the new pastor into the manse. They may be mired in the moment, uncertain where they want to go.

Consequently, an interview will determine whether this is God's call only when it reveals the real story, when through it we discover the heart of the congregation's expectations and hopes.

The Approach

Upon being invited to interview, I make it clear that I'll be asking a number of questions myself and that my questions will take at least an hour. I never assume that the search committee *expects* me to ask questions.

I was once the last of six candidates to interview with a particular church but the first to ask any questions. After our conversation, one committee member said, "We were surprised you had questions about coming here! We assumed our church was so attractive that any clergyman would be glad to come. I don't know if you're the right one for us, but you were the only candidate who forced us to think about what kind of minister our church needs."

In particular, there are three types of questions I try to raise:

Questions of *census* discover who the congregation is — the talents, skills, interests, and commitments these people bring to church. Questions of census also look beyond the congregation itself to the area it serves. Does the church draw its members from the surrounding community? Have there been major demographic shifts in the past ten years, and if so, how has the church addressed these shifts? Do these trends indicate future changes? Is housing in the area affordable for young couples? If not, what is the potential for church growth?

Every congregation also has particular *issues* I need to know about. Some are low-risk, pleasantly discussed questions of theory; others are powder kegs. Is the church inward or outward looking? Have changes in worship practice disrupted the congregation? Was there (or is there) any contention over the previous pastor? Have there been theological or other divisions in the congregation? Has a building program alienated anyone?

Just as questions of census cannot be divorced from the community at large, neither can questions of issues. Has the school district been affected by busing? Is the community racially, economically, and socially integrated? If so, is the congregation? Are crime rates increasing? Candidates must explore the social context to understand issues within the church.

Questions centering on *structures* attempt to discover both the formal and the informal (hidden) networks in the congregation. But they also can probe beyond the congregation. Are relations with neighboring churches friendly? Has this church been involved with ecumenical worship, educational, or fellowship programs? Are there strong ties between this congregation and the district, presbytery, or diocese? If the congregation is nonaligned, is there an active clergy association in the community for fellowship and support?

The interview is the time for hard and honest statements. If I expect the church to increase my salary by 15 percent every year, this is the time to say so. If I will be disappointed by a midweek service of less than 50 percent of the congregation, I ought to explain that in the interview.

In the same way, I need to elicit the committee's heart-felt, unwritten, but concrete expectations. Do they expect an eighty-hour work week? Do they expect me to be involved in the local community? The selection committee cannot represent all the congregational expectations, but they will probably suggest trends.

In addition, we must consider the relationship of our spouse to the interview process. Many clergy bristle when asked if their spouse will accompany them on the interview. Terse statements are frequently made ("You are hiring me, not my wife!"), which, while true, do not endear us to search committees.

Personally, I consider my wife a tremendous asset at a job interview. She has the ability to discern attitudes while I am embroiled in answering questions. In addition, she enjoys having the opportunity to meet the individuals involved — after all, she will have to live with them, too!

Before the Committee

As the interview begins, I ask if we might begin with prayer (if someone else has not already done so). If I pray, I let my prayer speak to the situation; I don't try to impress them with my ability at extemporaneous praying. One honest "Lord Jesus, quiet our anxious hearts" will do more than an eloquent "Almighty and Everlasting God, we beseech thee of thy manifold and gracious favors. . . ."

I believe both candidates and committee are best served if the committee ask their questions first. That way, I can modify my questions to follow up on issues they have raised. My agenda includes not only my concerns but also ministering to their needs.

I usually preface my questions with a statement that some answers I am looking for are matters of fact, but others are matters of feeling, specifically their feelings. As a result, I realize there may be different answers to one question, and I welcome that diversity of opinion.

I find it helpful to have a list of prepared questions based on my understanding of the congregation, rather than appearing to ask questions off the cuff. The best kind of spontaneity, someone once said, is the well-planned kind.

While I may be tempted to deal with specific events, statistics, and services, I resist the urge to focus on too narrow an area. While there are no perfect "canned" questions for each interview, I take the following approach. Some questions may be useful as stated; others will need modification depending on the situation.

The primary purpose is to let me hear committee members express their attitudes and expectations. I have found it far more helpful to understand their likes and dislikes than their financial condition for the last ten years.

Questions to Ask

Why am I of particular interest to you?

I start with this question. I am not fishing for compliments, but it helps to know if they're excited about me as their potential pastor. I also need to know why I am of real interest. The answer often surprises me.

I interviewed with one congregation who confessed (after I asked) that they weren't really interested, but the bishop had asked them to contact me, and they felt obliged to do so. Once I knew that, I was able to focus completely on their needs. In fact, we were able to talk in depth about their situation. As a result, they clarified some issues in their congregation's life, issues they had not recognized prior to my visit.

What has been the most significant event in the life of this congregation since you have been a member?

The question serves two purposes. First, I discover what events are significant to them, which helps both me and the committee focus on future expectations. In addition, I see what ministries this congregation considers significant. Do their responses focus on worship activities? Social functions? Outreach programs? Would I characterize any of those events as significant if they happened in my church?

Aside from the upheaval of looking for a new pastor, what has been the most upsetting event in the life of this church?

Unless this congregation is highly unusual, there has probably never been a public opportunity for members to express their frustration, disappointment, and anger. While they may have had plenty of private (and potentially divisive) opportunities, this question allows them to voice their pain openly. It also lets me know what is likely to upset them in the years ahead.

In your opinion, what areas of concern need to be addressed by this congregation?

Delightfully nonspecific, this question may be the perfect invitation for a committee member to open an issue that is unresolved or unrecognized. I must be prepared, however, to bring the group back to my agenda should they spend too much time on isolated concerns.

This question once evoked a heated argument within one search committee over a question of property maintenance. When we pursued it further, I discovered fully half the members expected the pastor to mow the church lawn in summer and shovel the snow in winter.

What kinds of things did your former pastor do particularly well?

Certain questions regarding predecessors are fair territory as long as I refer to them with respect and treat their ministries with courtesy and honor. In fact, if I'm kind in asking this question, it is appreciated. It allows those present to celebrate their former pastor in a specific way — by holding up his or her particular gifts in ministry. It also allows me to see what aspects of my predecessor's ministry were well received, including tasks that may be expected of me.

What were the circumstances surrounding your former pastor's departure?

I may already know the answer, having heard it through the grapevine. But unless the former pastor died in office, I find it helpful to let the committee state openly the reasons from their perspective. If my predecessor did die in office, or if he or she was extremely popular and moved on to another congregation, I will have to be sensitive to the committee's need to mourn. If I am following an individual who had a long term as pastor, I may want to ask if the committee feels another long-term pastorate is feasible considering the tenure of the predecessor.

In what areas did you wish your former pastors had more expertise?

"We've had three preachers in a row in this church, and now we need a money man!" Listening to this response by a committee member a few years ago, I felt glad I had asked!

I cushion this question by making the subject plural, thus taking the onus off the predecessor, but I still allow people to express their opinions about unaddressed areas of need.

Two caveats should be issued: First, I am not talking about personality traits but ministerial skills. Second, I ask people to speak only about first-hand experience. Rumors that pastor Smith didn't deal with poor Mr. Jones's suicide very well may be nothing more than that — rumors — and are therefore counterproductive.

What formal and informal methods of support have you used in the past to help your pastor become a better minister?

This question may stop them cold! If they display signs of confusion, I explain that I need congregational support. Did they encourage (and offer to pay for) any continuing education? Are there formal structures to assist the pastor in preaching by providing disciplined feedback? Has the congregation developed methods to evaluate their own performance as Christian ministers?

Tell me about the governing board.

And I mean everything! How are they elected? How frequently? Does the board rotate membership on a regular basis? What is the background, business, and interest of each member? What kind of jobs do they hold? Are they employers or employees? (The answer makes a significant difference in how they treat their clergy!)

Who runs the stewardship, Christian education, youth, mission, and outreach programs? Who oversees building maintenance? Is the church board bound to any state laws in addition to congregational by-laws and denominational procedures? If there is a staff in addition to the pastor, who is responsible for church-staff relations? How much authority does the board exercise in staff management? How frequently does the board meet? How long, on average, do the meetings last?

The church building may be beautiful, the community ideal, the manse a mansion, but the quality of our working life will be determined largely by our relationship with the board. So before I consider accepting a call, I discover as much as I can about its members and how they function.

Has the pastor's family traditionally taken an active role in this church?

In answering this question, committee members may reveal how they felt about the level of activity of previous pastors' families. Therein lies the key to the criteria by which my family will be judged.

How is the pastor's compensation package determined? How frequently is it reviewed? By whom? What factors are used in determining that package? Merit or cost-of-living increases? Social Security reimbursement? Equity in the parsonage or a cash equity allowance? Continuing education, book, and automobile allowances?

By this point, I usually know what salary the church is offering. What interests me now is whether I will participate in my salary review a year after my call. I also need to sensitize the committee to the increasing financial burden placed on clergy by factors beyond their control such as Social Security increases and the loss of equity by living in church-owned housing.

Far too often, humility (or embarrassment) prevents clergy from honestly discussing financial needs, but the laborer is worthy of his hire, and my compensation package must meet the needs of my family. My interest in the process and participation in annual reviews must be stated at the outset.

How should your pastor spend his or her time? In the course of a week, how much time should be spent in prayer? Personal study? Sermon preparation? Administration? Individual and family counseling? Visiting? With the family?

At some point, I get specific information about their expectations of my time. I remember asking a question about the rector's personal time, and a vestryman responded, "Day off? Why, our rectors never take a day off!" I accepted the call to that church and found the man wasn't kidding; they expected their rector to be available at a moment's notice. It took two years before they became accustomed to my practice of leaving town a day and a half each week.

How many hours do they expect me to work in a week? If I expect to work forty, and they expect eighty, better to know it now! How are those hours to be used? When they are used up and work remains undone, what happens? If I work extra hours one week, will they allow me to take those hours for myself and my family the next week? Do they see prayer, study, and sermon preparation as part of my work week or things to be done on top of forty hours of hospital and home visiting?

As I question, I try not to sound judgmental; my tone suggests that I am merely acquiring information. They may have thought of the pastor's job only in the most general terms. These questions force them to state their expectations clearly both for themselves and the candidate.

What organizations in the congregation are the most active or successful?

This allows me to determine congregational priorities. If the Ladies' Bridge Club is thriving but the Young People's Fellowship is limping along, I know where the interest and commitment is. I also ask if any organizations have dissolved in the last two years. If so, why?

Beyond calling a pastor and its related concerns, what is the highest congregational priority for the next twelve months?

Whatever the responses (and there are bound to be more than one), they will form my expected agenda for the next year. I must determine if their interests align with mine. I may want to build a men's program or start an emergency food cupboard, but they may want to panel the church lounge or pave the parking lot.

What goals have you established for church growth? What methods can be used to achieve those goals?

The question of growth is a census question. Where will the new people come from? If this community is like most others, the question will be how to attract and sustain the unchurched. Is the church ready for that?

Perhaps the most honest response I ever received to this question came from one committee member who said, "Getting more people is your job, and I don't care how you do it. I just come here to worship."

While undoubtedly many people feel this way, if that attitude is embraced by the congregation as a whole, the task before me will be formidable.

What plans have you made for the expansion of staff or buildings?

If they haven't planned for expansion, they don't intend to grow. The vision of their future ministry is bound by the limitations of the present moment. While this may not deter me from accepting a position, I realize I have some hard work cut out ahead, beginning with an expansion of their horizons.

How financially stable is this congregation?

Even in the best of economic times, few churches are able to work toward future financial security. So I ask them to speculate aloud about the future financial needs of the congregation.

What programs do you plan to implement in the next ten years?

Many churches feel any plans they may have had go out the window when a new pastor comes. On the other hand, some congregations may be anxious to implement changes the former pastor disallowed. This question allows them to state their dreams for the future. I, in turn, can give them an honest assessment of my interest in those particular programs, and with relatively little risk.

But How Do I Know?

The search for the perfect congregation is futile. No church can ever fully meet a minister's needs, any more than one minister can fulfill all the expectations of a congregation. Even so, I need not accept every offer that comes along. How do I know when to pursue an interview to the next stage or to accept the call if offered?

Accepting a call is at best a series of tradeoffs. I have to ask myself: *Am I willing to live with this particular drawback in order to acquire that specific benefit?*

Consequently, *before* we begin the process, we should take time to assess our professional needs and our family's social and economic needs. We need to ask such questions as:

What are the nonnegotiables? What are things I'd be willing to wait two years for? What are mere preferences? Do I have skills as a teacher that I need to use? Am I particularly gifted in youth work? Do I hunger to share my spiritual journey with a group of fellow pilgrims? What family needs will shape my decision? Will my spouse expect or need to work? What stage have my children reached in their schooling? Will their gifts or needs require specialized instruction or guidance?

In addition, we are wise to list areas where we will require assistance: Do I find administrative work a burden and hope to have members of the congregation share the load? Do I depend on lay assistance in visitation? Do I need structured feedback to help me gauge my performance?

An honest assessment of needs highlights specific areas the interview must address. If my needs assessment is carefully done, I'll know what I require and what I'm willing to trade off.

The criteria I establish, however, may not be my final basis for deciding. I once interviewed with a church that presented me with a dozen reasons to say no. Some members of the search committee were guarded, others hostile. Several questions I asked received an answer I didn't expect (or want). Accepting the call would have meant taking a cut in salary and moving my wife and children even farther from our already distant families. I was certain the pastor who accepted this call would be faced with a long list of difficulties.

But I accepted that call nonetheless and served that congregation many years. Sometimes a sense of God's call overpowers us, so that we feel compelled to follow. In that case, these questions are asked not to determine a call, but to understand how we will enter it.

The interview, then, as stressful and upsetting as it may be, is the best forum for hammering out concerns, commitments, and priorities. The atmosphere is intense; expectations and hopes are high. But if handled carefully and prayerfully, the interview process can be a time of joyous discovery that leads to a long and fruitful relationship.

The immediate goal of coming to terms is to make certain everybody understands the arrangement — the same arrangement. The long-term goal is to be able to work together happily for years to come.

— Ed Bratcher

CHAPTER THREE
Coming to Terms

By the time a search committee makes their selection and the pastoral candidate has agreed, in theory at least, to come to a church, a long process has been concluded. At this point, however, a shorter but equally vital process is about to begin. It's time to talk about the terms of call.

Throughout the interview process, committee and candidate have each expressed their ideas and concerns. As they've come closer and closer to an agreement, they've made more and more assumptions based on what they've learned about each other. Coming to terms is, in part, the process of transforming those assumptions into assurances.

When we get to this point, we feel we're talking with friends. We've come to know the search committee during the "courtship" period. These good people represent the congregation we expect to pastor soon. So we naturally want this coming to terms to feel more like a family discussion than a union bargaining session.

The immediate goal is to make certain everybody understands the arrangement — the *same* arrangement. The long-term goal is to be able to work together happily for years to come. Here are some things I kept in mind during this crucial last stage of the candidating process.

Some Friendly Business

Often the committee initiates this process and goes through the terms of the call as they understand them. Sometimes, however, we may need to formalize these assumptions ourselves, by saying something like, "For both of our sakes, let's make sure we have this all worked out. I need to know your expectations for this call, and you probably want to know mine. Could we work through some items about the call?" The point is: make sure the process is begun.

However initiated, I like this meeting to be conducted in a businesslike manner while retaining a friendly atmosphere. It works better, for example, when people are comfortably sitting on couches rather than nervously eyeballing one another across a table.

This conversation also works best with the search committee, rather than a personnel committee or church board, which are usually relatively unfamiliar with us as candidates. The search committee has been our primary contact with the church. They ought to be the ones who work out the arrangements with us. In situations in which the search committee's authority is limited, the committee can at least take the arrangements to the official board for approval or negotiation.

If we ask for unusual or extraordinary considerations, however, another committee should be brought in. For example, if the previous pastor received significantly less salary than the committee proposes I receive, I'd suggest, "Since this amount is decidedly more than what you had originally considered, it might be good for us to talk to the finance committee." We want to be sure the search committee has the full support of the congregation.

Avoiding the Adversarial

Since we want to begin our relationship with a congregation on a warm, nonadversarial tone, it's a mistake, I feel, to enter discussions with dogmatic expectations.

Rather than declaring my needs, I liked to begin the talks by asking for information. For instance, say I'm talking about continuing education opportunities. Instead of declaring, "I must have two weeks continuing education and $500 per year," I would ask the committee, "What has been your previous experience with continuing education?"

This is especially important when the church has had a bad experience in the area being discussed. If, in the example above, the previous pastor had used continuing education to sit on a Florida beach, the church would naturally be reticent about study leaves.

But when I ask, "What do you think about continuing education?" the committee can relate their bad experience. Then I can remain sensitive to their concerns, saying, for instance, "I certainly can see why a continuing education leave has left a bad taste in your mouths. But let me say why I consider study leave important *and* what I intend to do with any time you might give me."

This approach isn't aggressive, but it does allow me to get my concerns on the table. If I feel continuing education is crucial for my development as a minister, I'm setting myself up for disappointment and anger if I don't bring it up. It's like marrying and then trying to iron out differences over whether or not to have children. It doesn't work. *After* I become their pastor shouldn't be the first time they hear about my strong desire for continuing education.

In short, I approach this part of these negotiations neither dogmatically nor passively, but like this: "Here are some of the things important to me, and as we move along in this pastoral relationship, let's continue to talk about them. I trust you to do the right thing." Even if I have to give on some points, I leave open the possibility of further consideration down the road.

A related problem to avoid is entering the discussion with a long and detailed list of expectations. I've heard the counsel, "You're borrowing trouble if you don't make your needs known in a detailed and specific way. You and the church need to know exactly what to expect from each another." That's true to a certain extent, since there's no use obfuscating arrangements that need to be clear. But when it's taken too far, trust is undermined, and only a binding contract remains.

This is more likely to happen when one of the parties has been burned previously. Having had difficulties with their previous pastor, one church detailed to the point of absurdity the covenant with their next pastor. It contained pages of regulations such as: "The pastor will be present for and take a leadership role in Vacation Bible School," spelling out one by one all the duties their previous pastor had neglected.

Pastors who have been hurt are tempted to do the same thing. But that's not the way to begin a relationship amicably. It's fighting old wars with people we intend to be our allies.

Some Details We Do Need

While we don't want too detailed or dogmatic a list, we do want to achieve clarity and understanding as we come to terms. What details, other than reimbursement, we want to put into writing depends on our unique concerns. But one example will suggest that some fine details need to be ironed out ahead of time, because surprises down the road rarely are pleasant.

Let's say I move to a new church soon after Easter, not an unusual time for a pastoral transition. Arriving at the new church in April, I don't have many weeks before the kids are out of school, and it's time for a family vacation. But since I've been at the church only a couple of months, can I take a vacation that summer?

I need to bring up that possibility as part of the negotiations before I'm officially called to the church. Some churches don't allow a vacation until after twelve months of service. I don't want to learn that after our station wagon has been packed for the beach.

When coming to terms it's better to say to the committee, "Our family has made plans to spend two weeks at the beach in July. This is important to us, but I'll have been at the church only three months by then. Would there be any problem with my taking that time away?"

So a few details need attention. We should assume nothing about those things that are important to us.

Remuneration Ruminations

Central to the terms of call is remuneration. But before getting into details, we should be aware of the many factors that determine remuneration.

For example, the previous pastor's salary often sets limits on how much the church is willing to pay the new minister, at least at the beginning of his or her pastorate.

Then again, what other ministers earn can be a greater factor still. Although one congregation I served had been financially gracious to me, they found that after I left, the salary I'd been given didn't match what pastors candidating for the position were receiving. Finally the search committee had to approach the congregation, saying, "Folks, we won't be able to talk seriously with the kind of pastor we want based on what we paid Ed." The church agreed and raised the salary package.

Churches sometimes set the pastor's salary close to the mean or median salary in the congregation, thinking the pastor should live on the level of the average member. Another rule of thumb is to look at the pay of comparable professionals in the community, such as a high school principal, for example.

Naturally, the size and budget of a church also sets limits on what churches, no matter how well intentioned, can realistically afford.

Two factors to be weighed carefully are first, the needs of the pastor (size of family, children in college, etc.), and second, the compensation of other pastors of similar churches in the community. Earnings vary considerably by denomination and by church, but I like to make people aware of what other local congregations are paying.

Finally, although most congregations have determined more or less what they'll pay a pastor, the search committee and candidate can apportion the dollars within the pay package. Creative and personalized distribution of the gross pay can satisfy both the church's desire to be fair but thrifty, and the pastor's need to maximize the utility of the gross pay.

A Package of Many Parts

To see how, in fact, pay can be apportioned, let's look at four major components of a salary package.

● *Salary.* It's important for laypeople that we keep salary distinct from reimbursements and benefits. Laypeople often look at the total budget for the pastor (which usually includes reimbursements such as car allowance, benefits such as pension dues and health insurance, but does not include self-employment social security tax), divide it by twelve, and compare that figure with their own monthly take-home pay. Of course, we come out looking overpaid.

Salary is what we must live on. Therefore the salary portion of our pay package needs to remain distinct from reimbursements for expenses we accrue by doing ministry: mileage costs for hospital calls, long-distance church calls from home, dinner out with the guest evangelist, and so on. Salary is what we're paid; reimbursements pay us back for costs that ought not come from our pockets.

In most churches, our salary figure is tied closely to our housing figure, because the two categories together constitute what is salary for nonclergy. When a congregation does not provide us a parsonage, it's not uncommon for pastors to divide the total salary into portions for salary and housing allowance that best fit their needs. The cost to the church remains the same, but our tax advantages can be significant.

While talking salary, it's a good idea to make clear when and how salary reviews will take place. Will they be yearly? What criteria will be used? Who initiates the review, and who will conduct it? Since living costs continue to rise yearly, some provision for regular salary review is important.

We don't have to pin down a church to specific details about the salary review, such as expected percentages. But we can show we expect people to treat us equitably year by year.

● *Housing.* Two arrangements are common: (a) a house (parsonage) provided free by the congregation, or (b) a housing allowance paid to us to secure housing of our choice. Since the value of the parsonage or the money given in a housing allowance is not taxable for income tax purposes (although it is for self-employment taxes), the provision of housing is, in effect, an income-tax-free segment of our salary. We pastors gain a great benefit from this provision, and we are wise to convert as much as possible of our salary/housing payment into housing, given, of course, the limitations placed by the IRS.

If paid a housing allowance, generally we are wise to make the allowance large enough to cover expenses for buying (or renting) a residence, furnishing it, maintaining it, paying for utilities, and even purchasing cleaning or maintenance supplies for it. If necessary, we're ahead if we give up a little salary to obtain a larger housing allowance, as long as we can justify the housing allowance to the IRS. In fact, when determining the housing allowance (or other tax-related items), it's wise to check with a tax accountant knowledgeable about clergy taxes.

A person just getting started in ministry may find a parsonage the better plan. First, that may make possible a somewhat larger cash salary. Second, the pastor can move right in, rather than search for a home during the hectic relocation time. Most often, the church pays for the utilities or provides a utility allowance for the pastor.

If pastors use a parsonage, they need to make clear with the committee which responsibilities are the pastor's and which the church's. Specifically, can we decorate the parsonage, or do we need permission for any changes? Who pays for redecoration? Who fixes a leaky faucet, and do we need someone's approval to call a plumber? Who pays the utilities? These kinds of agreements are important, because pastors sometimes have found themselves in hot water, so to speak, by not knowing the standard procedure.

One distinct disadvantage of a parsonage, however, is that upon retirement the pastor won't have equity in a home. One way to remedy that situation is for the parsonage-dwelling pastor to request that money be set aside each month for a housing fund that he or she will receive at retirement.

An Episcopal rector I knew in Manassas worked an agreement with his congregation whereby they contributed $125 a month and he added from his pay another $100 a month to a Tax-Sheltered Annuity in his name, so that by retirement he will have built a fund toward purchasing his own home. He has since been called to another congregation, but the annuity went with him and will be available when he retires. He and his new church can continue to build the annuity, if they so choose.

● *Benefits.* Although not exactly pay, benefits certainly enhance the pay package and often add up to a significant percentage of actual salary and housing. Therefore, it's a good policy to discuss exactly which benefits will be provided by the church. The possibilities are considerable:

— Retirement plan. Retirement has a way of sneaking up on a pastor, and it's never too early to get started on retirement planning. For the most part, churches want their pastors to be well cared for in retirement, and many denominations and associations encourage churches and pastors to participate in pension plans. My denomination, for instance, suggests setting aside 10 percent of income in their retirement plan.

The government recently has encouraged personal retirement investment through Tax-Sheltered Annuities, known as 403(b) plans, for employees of nonprofit organizations. In these plans the employer deducts money from salary and deposits it directly into an annuity. So it is good to talk with the search committee to see if this plan can be made available. Any portion of our salary thus taken from our pay to be saved for retirement is not taxable until we start withdrawing it upon retirement, so we save on current taxes while preparing for retirement.

— Health insurance. This is practically a must in today's

world. If the church doesn't provide it as a benefit, most of us will find it necessary to pay for it out of pocket. If we can get it included as a benefit (even if we have to give up a little salary to do so), we may be able to save a little on taxes, depending on how exactly we itemize our deductions.

— Disability insurance. I consider disability coverage tremendously important. Since it often isn't automatically included in a pay package, it's well worth negotiating.

When I was a pastor in Austin, Texas, a local pastor of a smaller congregation fell down some stairs at his church and was left paralyzed. He didn't have disability insurance, but the church wanted to be fair with him, so they continued his salary for many months. Finally, however, they needed to call another pastor, and they couldn't afford the salary of two pastors. It became a tragic, no-win situation.

— Life insurance. Term life and mortgage insurance don't cost a congregation much and can give a lot of peace of mind. I recommend looking into them as benefits. Regular life insurance, which is more of a personal investment, is something I've taken care of personally.

● *Expense accounts.* I feel the cost of doing ministry ought to be borne by the church. Therefore, we need to make clear with the search committee just which expenses will be picked up by the congregation — and how payment will be made.

Under today's tax laws, generally it is beneficial for pastors to voucher professional expenses and be reimbursed by the church, rather than receive from the church a set allowance and then pay one's own expenses from the allowance. As long as we document carefully our expenses under the first system, the IRS considers our expenses and reimbursements a "wash." But if we receive a set allowance, we'll end up paying taxes on the portion of it we cannot deduct as professional expenses.

For this reason, I recommend setting up with the church a system for presenting documented expenses (who, what, when, ministry purpose, etc.) and being reimbursed by the treasurer. That way the church — not you — foots the bill for genuine costs of your doing ministry, and you don't pay taxes on the part of your money that goes toward paying professional expenses.

Here are some expenses you may want to discuss with the committee:

— Transportation costs. According to the IRS, commuting costs aren't professional expenses, so we can't expect reimbursement for driving to and from church. But as pastors, we use a car to do visitation, make hospital calls, attend meetings, and drive for youth events. That mileage adds up, and most churches are willing to foot the bill.

A car allowance is one way churches can repay us for our expenses, but tax experts recommend against it, since we must pay taxes on a portion of it. Two other systems require a little record keeping yet fully reimburse our expenses. Under the first system, we keep a log of our ministry miles and get reimbursed on a per-mile basis, currently 26 cents a mile. The second system demands that we keep track of our actual expenses (gas, repairs, depreciation, insurance, etc.) and our ministry and personal mileage; then we submit a request for reimbursement for the ministry proportion of our expenses. That plan has worked best for me, mainly because of the depreciation schedule.

— Continuing education. Many churches want to encourage the professional development of their pastor, so they budget money each year to cover the pastor's costs for attending seminars and meetings. Some churches even put aside money yearly to fund a sabbatical for the pastor.

— Books and periodicals. Building a good library costs money. Churches may want to help pay these professional costs through a book account from which we can draw to purchase commentaries and other tools of the trade. Again, a vouchered account has the best tax advantages.

— Other expenses. Pastors accrue other expenses in the course of ministry. When my wife and I had to take a guest minister and his wife to dinner, it could easily cost forty dollars. Or when I took the Manassas church secretaries to lunch for Secretaries' Week, it got expensive to pick up the tab. Other pastors join Rotary Club as a community ministry for the church. If churches are to cover these costs, it needs to be agreed upon in advance.

— Moving expenses. The costs of a move are considerable, and although some can be deducted from taxes, that deduction doesn't begin to cover the costs. Churches most often will make arrangements to help substantially with the move, but we can't just assume that.

Also, *how* the move is made is important. Are we expected to move ourselves, with help unloading at our new community? Do we hire professional movers and bill the church? Will the church pick up the costs of a professional move, up to a certain dollar figure? These questions need to be ironed out. And since most movers require a substantial deposit, how that is to be paid must also be decided.

Delineating Other Agreements

Other questions that have little to do with money need answers. Most of these questions revolve around working arrangements. Consider the following:

• *Job description.* A pastor's job is nearly impossible to put on paper. How do you chart a pastor's vision? Yet a general statement of the responsibilities of the job can help formalize what both parties consider important.

For instance, pastors need to know to whom they are answerable and whom they supervise. That's basic. In my church in Waynesboro, I knew the minister of music and youth supervised the organist, and the minister of education supervised the custodian. But the church secretary reported directly to me, as did the financial secretary. Knowing these formal relationships helped me as I began pastoring that church; I didn't accidently step on another supervisor's toes.

Any pastor entering a unique position or who expects to minister in ways out of the ordinary ought to have the particulars spelled out in a job description. I know of a Church of God pastor who feels his primary call is to be an evangelist, so his job description makes clear that he won't be responsible for some typical pastoral duties, such as crisis counseling. That church has made other arrangements to cover that area. Since it's clearly spelled out in the job description and everybody agrees, it hasn't caused a problem.

• *Performance reviews and termination.* Many pastors are suspicious of performance reviews. Sometimes it seems that churches perform reviews only when people are critical of the pastor. Furthermore, pastors feel few people are qualified to review their work. But I found reviews a helpful process. I felt that if I was going to have an effective ministry, I needed to hear how my ministry was being received.

Therefore, I found it helpful at least yearly to talk with the board of deacons about (1) what had been most meaningful to them in the church in the last year, and (2) what they would like to see happen in the church. Pastors are wise to work out some system of review in the terms of call.

Forced termination has become more common these days, and that makes it important for us to be acquainted with the church's policy for termination. Some churches have no such policy, and in that case, it may be a good idea eventually to place something in the bylaws.

It is not uncommon for the termination policies to stipulate the notice that should be given by either party wanting to terminate the pastoral agreement. Other matters such as continued use of the parsonage, salary continuation, and references often are covered.

• *Vacation and study leave.* I like to have a clear understanding about the number of vacation days I am given each year. Since pastors' weeks evolve differently from other professionals, vacation days can become confusing. For instance, what does "four weeks of vacation" mean? Twenty-eight days in a row? Four Sundays plus twenty-four other assorted days away? Should I take it all at once, or am I expected to spread it out a little? These things can be cleared up in discussion with the search committee.

Likewise, study leave for continuing education needs to be agreed upon. Many churches recognize the validity of time away for concerted study and even encourage it. But not all churches, so I need to know which kind of church I'm coming to. And can I accumulate study leave for a few years and take a major break? Can I accumulate the continuing education allowance, if there is one?

And how about a sabbatical? The beginning of the relationship is often the easiest time to request a sabbatical. After all, it remains six or seven years in the future. It's easy to grant when it's so far away!

● *Other considerations.* Pastors often have idiosyncratic needs that ought to be discussed. Perhaps the pastor doesn't want his children in the local school district, so he won't be living particularly close to the church. Or maybe a pastor wants to write, which might take some time away from the local ministry. During one period, I was interested in pastor-church relations and sometimes taught classes in seminary or spoke at conferences. I wanted my church to know that. These individual requests and needs ought to come out in the open. It's better to get permission early on than later to have to seek forgiveness.

Another consideration is the involvement of the spouse, if the pastor is married. The view that the spouse is an unpaid associate pastor is dying a slow death in the church, yet most pastoral spouses today prefer to set their own level of involvement. And many choose or need to be employed outside the home. Knowing the church's mind on such issues is important as we start a ministry.

For instance, my wife preferred not to attend Sunday school at my last church, and some people found that difficult to accept, although she was active in many other areas of church life. I had made it clear in the interview, however, that I hoped Marjie would be treated no differently than any other church member, and the search committee had concurred with me. Thus, although we didn't convince some church members, we had only minimal trouble with her decision.

Continuing the Discussion

In the churches I've served, I've asked the search committee not to dissolve until I've been in the church a year. These people were my first and most significant contacts with the church. I've known pastors who felt abandoned in the new church after the search committee disbanded, but I enjoyed a group of people who helped ease me into the culture of the church as well as tackle problems I faced.

Upon assuming my duties in one church, I discovered, to my surprise, that the church had some serious financial problems. I hadn't been told of that possibility by the search committee. So I went to them and said, "Now, I understood the church to be in good financial shape. I'm beginning to get another picture from the finance committee. Help me out. Did I understand you wrong?"

It turned out the committee was also surprised by our difficulties. The finance committee, wanting not to disturb the congregation during a crucial time, had kept the problems to themselves until they had a new pastor. Calling the committee together to clear up the question kept me from feeling betrayed by them.

In another instance, though, I was the one who had failed to hear something the search committee had said. But in any case, it was valuable to be able to go back to the committee I knew best to work out such misunderstandings.

And that, finally, is the point of coming to terms tactfully yet honestly. We want to avoid misunderstandings, hurt feelings, and major conflicts. We want to set up a framework that allows us to work well together for years to come.

PART TWO
Making a Move

I've gradually learned how to leave properly, so that with the tension there is also a sense of joy.
— *Robert Kemper*

CHAPTER FOUR

Preparing to Leave

The fable of the race between the tortoise and the hare reminds me of when I've accepted a new call. It's not so much the unexpected outcome of the race or the moral about tenacity or the warning about overconfidence that impresses me. It's just that when I accept a new pastorate, I feel like *both* a tortoise and a hare.

As he moves, the tortoise carries with him everything he owns, with the consequent risk that entails. I am amused by *The New Yorker* magazine cartoon depicting a turtle with a hung-over look on his face. The caption says, "What a night. Hailstones!" Such are the complications of self-contained units.

After deciding to move, there comes a moment in the moving process, whether I am loading a U-Haul trailer or professionals are filling up a huge Allied van, when I see all my worldly possessions strewn upon my front lawn. To me that's not only a dramatic symbol of what is taking place in my life, it reminds me how vulnerable I am at such moments — like the cartoon turtle in *The New Yorker*.

Then again, after receiving a new call, I also feel like the hare. The hare, of course, represents speed. Likewise, after taking a new call, I instantly become future-oriented. My whole being moves toward what will be; the past and present become disproportionately smaller, and the future looms big and bright. I feel a great rush to get on with the future, or better, to get to the future. The present seems a barrier, an annoying distraction from what is really important to me. "Let's get going," says the rabbit in me.

In spite of such tensions, my three pastoral moves have been glad and celebrative experiences. There's something about closing one chapter of my life and opening myself to a new one that excites me.

Over my three moves, I've gradually learned how to leave properly so that with the tension there is also a sense of joy. Here are some of the principles I've found helpful.

Letting Emotions Have Their Way

Watching my daughter get married — that moment was filled with mixed emotions. On the one hand, I was sad that one era of my wife's and my relationship with our daughter was ending. On the other hand, it was the beginning of something fresh and wonderful for our daughter.

There are many experiences in life like that, where two contrary emotions struggle for predominance. Changing churches is one of them. At one moment, I feel terrific — a wonderful church wants me. I look forward to helping them move ahead in ministry for years to come. Then the next moment my 12-year-old daughter comes to me in tears, "Daddy, do we *have* to move?!" The ecclesiastical hero has become the family villain.

It's difficult to live back and forth between contrary emotions. For one thing, it wears me out. But if I try to fight these emotions, or simply suppress the negative in favor of the positive, I simply complicate the already complex situation and make myself more exhausted still. Consequently, I've found it better to let such emotions weave their way in my life, and let God, in his own time, resolve the tensions.

In particular, I have found great help in being able to talk with a ministerial friend, not just a colleague, but one who speaks my language, who lets me be myself, who often knows intuitively what I'm feeling. I like to talk with another human being without my having to paint the picture or qualify myself. To such a person I can say things aloud I do not really mean but need to say, and I can speak about my ambivalent feelings.

A Good Good-by

Moving means having to write a "Dear John" letter. Somehow I have to tell my congregation that I am leaving them for another.

Because it's so difficult, I've been tempted to make a clean break of it: "I hereby resign my pastorate effective December 31." Technically, that is all I have to say.

But then I begin to think of particular people in the parish: my golfing partners, the women at my baby's shower, the person who slipped me extra cash for a get-away vacation, the troubled ones who have trusted me and counted on my support. In addition, special memories crowd into my consciousness: the place my daughter was baptized; the budget battle we fought and won, despite the odds; the addition of a new Sunday school wing.

When such thoughts rush in, I feel as if I'm rejecting friends and renouncing treasured moments. And so that letter becomes harder and harder to write. I'm eager to tell these loved ones about my good news, but my good news will be bad news to them, and to me. At such times it's not unusual for me to wonder, *Am I doing the right thing?*

In composing the letter, then, I find it helpful simply to recognize the strong emotions that swirl within. Then exactly how to write the letter becomes easier in one sense: I simply tell people what's going on with me.

So I not only tell them what is happening, but how I'm struggling. I tell them how hard it is to make this decision, and how painful it is to leave a congregation that has been good to me. To me, that's the proper tone for a pastoral letter of resignation, not because it's the most diplomatic, but because it's the truest.

In addition, I also remind the congregation of the need for changes, that I cannot do everyone's funeral, confirm or baptize every child. I celebrate what has been good between us. I also name high accomplishments we've worked on jointly. Finally, I assure them that the church goes on. Paul used the phrase, "When Timothy comes. . . ." I've found that a useful analogy to employ; it helps the congregation get use to the idea of someone succeeding me.

Lyle Schaller also suggests that we include in this letter a variety of reasons for leaving: theological ("It's God's will"), professional ("The new church will use many of my gifts"), and personal ("We'll be within an hour of my wife's parents"), and the like. If we offer multiple reasons, members will surely understand at least one of the reasons we're leaving and so better accept our decision to move.

Ministering Until the Last

Until my resignation takes effect I am still the incumbent. I still have continuing duties, and in spite of my rabbit impatience to get on, I try to perform these duties with professional competence and integrity.

● *Special occasions.* Some of these routine duties take on a special urgency for the congregation. People want me to baptize a child, marry a daughter, or whatever, before I leave. Although such last-minute requests can crowd my calendar, I try to do as many as I can. They are testimonials to the congregation's regard for me, and I want to honor that.

● *Administrative urgencies.* Elected lay leaders feel a new sense of responsibility for the church when they know I will not be there to counsel them. So they ask many questions of procedure and propriety, sometimes in desperation.

There is a story about a fresh seminary graduate who, shortly after graduation, called the professor of practical theology to ask, "What do you do at a funeral?"

The professor was astounded. "We covered that in class," he said.

"Yes, I remember," said the graduate, "but this guy is *really* dead."

Something of that sort goes on with lay leaders when we resign. They have heard what to do, but faced with the prospect of having to do it themselves, they are in a bit of a panic.

One way I respond to this anxiety is by cranking up the special administrative machinery that will help the church find a pastoral successor. In my denomination that means meeting with our moderator, the chief lay officer of the congregation. I make sure the moderator, other church leaders, and denominational officers responsible for helping churches get in contact with one another.

In our case, the church council must nominate a search committee which, in turn, must be elected by the whole congregation. I often urge the moderator to make sure that many different parts of the congregation be represented on that committee, including youth. In that way everyone will feel their concerns are addressed in the selection of the new pastor.

Polities differ in how they find successors, of course, but I've followed one piece of advice given in all of them: I give no direction to the selection of a particular person to succeed me. My role is simply to teach them how to find a successor — of their choosing.

• *Private audiences.* Certain people need to meet with me personally and privately. No matter how I communicate my resignation, a few people (some with whom I'm close, others who may feel betrayed, others who are counting on me) are entitled to a private conversation about my move. In such conversations, I try to communicate my decision is not a personal rejection of them.

• *Reconciliations.* Then, there are those people who I've managed to alienate from the church during my tenure. In some cases I have to let bygones be just that. But sometimes one last stab at reconciliation is in order.

In one parish I served, we had a man and wife who were loyal parishioners and who also loved music. They had wanted our church to purchase a new organ. In what I thought was the best interests of the congregation, I had not supported their idea. They held that against me for the rest of my pastorate.

Before I left the parish, however, I made a call on that couple. I acknowledged they had probably felt hurt and disappointed in me for not supporting their cause. I told them I thought new ideas had to be good and timely, and that theirs had been good, but the time was not right. I cannot say that they were suddenly enlighted by this explanation, but we parted with a greater mutual respect.

It's More Gracious to Receive

Truly, it is more blessed to give, but it's more gracious to receive. So I try to anticipate and accept graciously the parting tributes of my parishioners.

First there are the gifts. People want and need to bid me farewell, and giving gifts is a way they do that. In addition, there is some sort of collective party at which a special gift is given — although I never anticipate exactly what! (When asked what I want at such parties, I simply ask that the occasion be celebrative and not maudlin.)

In addition, dinner and luncheon invitations abound. Sometimes I've found all this becomes a bit much. Parting festivities blur into one big mirage; I cannot remember who said what or what I did and did not do.

Nevertheless, the congregation and I *both* need this. The proper word for all these festivities is *closure*. Endings need to be formalized in some way. First, they mark the new chapter in my life. Second, they clear out debris for the church, so it can make a fresh beginning.

In addition, I've found that graciously receiving farewells prepares me to receive new welcomes. For me tears are part of farewells, even though most of the time I'd rather avoid tears. But when I shed no tears, I fail to acknowledge the permanence of the change. When no permanent change is acknowledged, I have a more difficult time starting up in my new place.

One caveat: when leaving a parish, I do not believe all the nice things said about me. I receive tributes graciously but also with a grain of salt. If I don't, I may wonder why I'm leaving these wonderful people in the first place, and I may convince myself that my new sense of call was nothing but indigestion.

Meanwhile Back at the Parsonage . . .

When I was 10 years old, my father, a pastor, received a new call. I remember my mother gathering a school party for me. My parting gift was an address book. At the party everyone entered their names and addresses that we might write to each other. It was a memorable gift, symbolically and in fact.

I also remember attending my parents' farewell reception and some dinner parties. In sum, as a 10-year-old, I was not excluded from the family's closure ceremonies. Further, my parents made a special effort to show me pictures and drawings of our new home. As a child, I needed to be assured there was a special place for me in the new and unknown environment.

In various ways, I need to recognize my family's needs at such a time. They need to experience closure, too. My wife will have farewells at her work, my children at their school. As often as possible, I like to share these experiences with them as they share mine with me.

I mentioned that poignant moment when, like the turtle, I see all my worldly possessions strewn out in front of me. Before I get to that moment, however, I'm tempted to vigorously and decisively eliminate some of those possessions: *No sense carrying around things we no longer use,* I think. For me, books especially are a case in point.

However, there is another side to this issue. Books, for example, are my professional tools, too powerful of a symbol to discard lightly. Nor should I be too quick to cast off my children's old toys; children too need symbols of continuity in the face of uncertain change. Just before a move, then, may not be the best time to simplify one's life.

"By faith, Abraham went forth from Ur of Chaldea. . . ." So he did. Clear. Simple. But the Bible does not say how Sarah felt about it. It does not mention the late-night conversations in the tent about whether to go. It does not show Abraham having to explain to neighbors where he was going and why. We don't see the hassles of changing addresses, negotiating with movers, filling out forms, and making deposits. We don't hear about the nitty-gritty of moving that can be a pain in the neck, not to mention heart rendering.

Of course, the Bible is right in focusing on the larger events, like the divine call to which we must respond. But moving also contains many little things, little concerns we are wise to attend to. When we do, it makes our dutiful obedience to God's call all the more joyful.

Accepting a new call does not have to mean two or three years of feeling (or playing) the stranger. By directing some thought and action before a move, we can quickly fasten the ties that bind.

— *Doug Scott*

CHAPTER FIVE

Moving Right In

My wife and I nervously looked right and then left as we scanned the pleasant tree-lined street for house numbers. The magic number was 92, the rectory of the church I had just been called to serve, but all we saw were dozens of seemingly numberless houses.

We were anxious for our first glimpse of the house we would call home. We had followed the moving van for 150 miles. The driver led us through a labyrinth of streets and back roads. *Friends will have to find us*, I thought. *I'll never be able to find my way out.*

The van stopped in front of a nondescript house with a leaf-strewn lawn. While there was nothing to distinguish it as a rectory (the church itself was about four miles away), the key was underneath the front mat, just as one of the board members had promised.

"There probably won't be anyone there to greet you," he had said. But someone had pinned a note to the front door saying, "Welcome to your new home!"

Busy hours passed, and when the truck was finally unloaded and the movers gone, Jane and I surveyed the impassable mountain of book boxes. Drawing herself out of her fatigue, she said, "Well, we better get to the supermarket or we'll die of starvation."

We both stood up and headed for the door. Then I stopped, and we looked at each other. Jane asked tentatively, "Do you know where the supermarket is?"

"I don't know where *anything* is."

With a flash of inspiration, I grabbed the telephone and juggled the handset while I fumbled in my wallet for the church phone number. I dialed, listened to three rings, then four, and then heard the cheery voice of the church secretary electronically proclaim, "There is no one here to help you now, but plan to come to church this Sunday and meet our new rector!"

They'd have to find me first.

Mobile Ministers

Clergy spend months talking with representatives of congregations about the possibility of a move, but all too often they deal almost exclusively with the acceptance of a job, not the relocation of a home. Among other things, this means that clergy families adopt the mentality of what theologians might call "pilgrim people," but everyone else calls "refugees."

For many families, the ministry demands that homes be disrupted, friendships distanced, and children stressed. Each move is painful since in almost every case it means leaving not just a job, but a home, schools, and a community. And, studies tell us, clergy do this every seven years or so. Only circus stars move more.

But given the necessary relocation associated with ministry, accepting a new call does not have to mean two or three years of feeling (or playing) the stranger. By directing some thought and action *before* a move, we can quickly fasten the ties that bind.

Before You Leave

The next time I relocated, the search committee and I had just finalized my call. We had begun to rehearse a long list of things, both ecclesiastical and practical, that had to be accomplished — notification of my current bishop and the bishop of the diocese to which I would be moving, the necessary paperwork, and all the moving arrangements. When the list making slowed, I said, "There's something you could send us that we believe is fairly important."

"Just name it," the chairman said cheerfully.

"Jane and I would like some anticipation."

"I beg your pardon?"

"We need some anticipation — you know, the best thing about Christmas or your birthday is the anticipation. You see, we will be here for another six weeks before we move into your rectory. Frankly, those weeks will be hard on us. Members of this congregation are already expressing their pain and disappointment at the prospect of our departure. We will have lots of painful farewells. Our life will be stashed in piles of cardboard boxes. We'll be feeling lonely and a little afraid. Now, it's true that I'll have a new job to look forward to, but the rest of my family needs a little more than that. We'd like you to send us something about our new home that we can look forward to."

"I hadn't thought of that," he said, "but now that you mention it, my wife and I felt pretty isolated when we moved into town seven years ago. Did you have anything specific in mind?"

Actually, I had something very specific in mind, which I believed would help not only Jane and me, but also the congregation.

"I'd be thrilled if you would take a few minutes with your wife and talk about the things you discovered when you first arrived, and jot them on a piece of paper," I said. "Then, if you think they might be willing to help, ask members of the congregation to share favorite places or pieces of helpful information. Give everyone a piece of paper after church and have them write one or two things they would want to know if they were new in town."

The response was overwhelming. We received recommendations for everything from the best hardware store to a hidden picnic spot in a local park, not to mention telephone numbers: the newspaper delivery service, three or four diaper services (Jane and I were moving toward our second child as well as a new church), babysitters, even a few notes saying, "This is my phone number. Call me anytime." In addition to getting valuable information that would have taken months to unearth by ourselves, the request gave us a feeling of instant assistance.

I've found clergy often feel like the distant stranger upon their arrival in a new setting. Feeling our first task is to move toward self-reliance as soon as possible, we ask only for patience as we struggle with names, and ready forgiveness when we make those inevitable first administrative mistakes.

But this request, unashamedly asking for help with the little things of daily life, gives the congregation opportunity to share its pride in its community. It also begins the pastoral relationship with an attitude of benevolent action. It's difficult for a congregation to "wait and see" skeptically when it has already offered care.

I also found that a short thank-you note to each person who wrote was more than politic. It was the first seed of relationship; it provided access immediately upon arrival. Even after we had been in that congregation a number of years, these associations remained strong ("We first ate in this restaurant because the Smiths suggested it").

Even more can be done. At one interview, I was presented with a loose-leaf notebook filled with photographs of the church, the rectory, nearby schools, playgrounds, shopping centers, and parks. There were pages with listings of movie theaters, restaurant reviews, a season schedule for the community theater, and bulletins from area churches. Two issues of the weekly paper were included, together with a few pages describing attractions in the nearest large city. Someone had included a coupon for a free car wash from a service station in town.

A new pastor could easily ask a congregation to provide many of these materials and more. After all, wouldn't you like to have a town map and telephone book *before* you really need them?

Matters of the Manse

In planning one move, I called the church warden and asked who was handling the cleaning and redecoration of the rectory. She sputtered for a few moments and then said, "Well, someone's swept the floors and cleaned the refrigerator, but that's all we were planning to do. We figured you would decorate the house after you arrived."

I cautiously asked, "Does that mean the church has funds set aside for us to do that?"

The silence seemed to last for hours.

"Well, frankly, no. We thought . . . "

Housing concerns are paramount in any transition, but they can be the most difficult issues to negotiate successfully during the time of call and move. Whether we live in church-owned housing or buy our own, it's wise to explore each other's expectations.

The issues may not seem that great if you're buying your own home, but I clearly remember the frantic call of a friend six weeks after his arrival in a new church. "The parish is in an uproar because we bought a house with a pool! I didn't even want the pool, but it was in the back yard of the house I liked. Now half the congregation is complaining that the board must be giving me an exorbitant housing allowance!"

"Are they really upset about the housing allowance?" I asked.

"No," he said quietly. "I found out two weeks after closing that I'm the only one in the congregation with a swimming pool."

Asking a few questions about congregational expectations before you look for a house certainly doesn't hurt (nor would a drive by the former pastor's house). Obviously, no one would suggest that church members have the right to dictate our choice of a home, but exploring attitudes is responsible and wise.

I suggested that my friend sponsor monthly parish pool parties during the summer months. Eventually these parties were heavily attended, and while they did nothing for his privacy, they did wonders for his popularity.

Those who live in church-owned housing might well be prepared for some compromise on the issue of redecoration. I live in a rectory where all the walls were painted white before we arrived. But as a tradeoff, we got to select the type and color of carpeting for the entire house.

The most important issue in the repair and redecoration of the parsonage, however, is not what happens when we arrive (when the congregation is filled with excitement at the prospect of our arrival), but rather when the church intends to repair and redecorate again. While negotiating variables like salary and benefits, I try to talk about the frequency with which I can expect the church to attend to the interior of the house.

Agreement on inspection and action every three to five years is fair to the pastor as well as important to the congregation if it is to maintain its investment. But like the other agreements that surround our employment, it's best to get it in writing. I try to have it added to my contract, not as an issue of trust but a matter of memory. After all, before many of these questions will be raised again, the entire board could easily rotate off, and the simple act of asking that the dining room be painted could become a strain.

"We never agreed to that!" an angry treasurer once bellowed at me. Because I was able to produce a contract that the church and I signed before he took office, I was spared the ugly necessity of defensiveness, and he was quickly corrected without debate.

Discovering Events

Church members have many expectations surrounding our arrival, and many will want to direct our "first burst." Which will it be — Sunday school reorganization, confirmation instruction, adult classes, property concerns?

"I don't think you understand. We have a lot of work to do here!" The woman, who looked at me over bulging vestry files stuffed with urgency, wasn't angry, just confused. They had saved a year's worth of clergy-must-see paper and expected that would be my first concern.

In addition to attending to the must-do pile, however, I feel my first and greatest task is to meet people. I must know them before I can minister to them. So at the very beginning of my ministry in a church, I've used our home to invite groups of ten to fifteen people over until the whole congregation and I have met face to face. However, I had to learn exactly what to seek during these evenings.

At first my plan for the content of these evenings was simple. I would tell them a little about my background and let Jane do the same. Then, in best church-conference fashion, we would move around the room and ask for name, neighborhood, employment, and number of years at this church. Then, I thought, I would ask a few leading questions and the discussion would begin.

As it turned out, while the plan was simple, it was also naive. At the end of the first evening, Jane and I agreed that the conversation had been sparse. I had worked hard just to keep the discussion focused. I admitted I was uncomfortable with the prospect of spending another fifteen evenings like that.

"I know what happened," Jane said. "They don't trust you enough to open up about their church life. After all, it is one of the most intimate relationships we have. And it may not have been just you. Don't forget that just because they live in the same area doesn't mean they're friends. That may have been a room filled with strangers. Those folks might have simply seen each other across a pew every week for years."

I was convinced she was right. And after a day of thought and discussion, a few members of the vestry and I came up with a new approach for the house meetings. We agreed the format should be social, conversational, and light. After all, we wanted to start a friendship, not bring it to completion. The information we would ask for would not be about feelings and opinions, but about *events*.

These were the key to our common life.

Within a short time, we had devised a full page of questions people would enjoy answering. We had even concocted a silly "take a question with your coffee" game that made each person a participant.

The next evening, people delighted in giving two or three answers to such questions as:

"What was the funniest thing to happen at a worship service?"

"What wedding here was the most beautiful?"

"Which Christmas pageant contained the most mistakes?"

"What has been the saddest moment in the life of this church since you have been a member?"

"Which former members do you miss the most? Why?"

As the night went on and one story led to another, we discovered we were talking not only about our congregation, but about other churches around the world as people shared their histories with one another. While this may not have made us close friends yet, we had begun to know and trust one another.

All in the Family

At these meetings, I also took about ten minutes to explain clearly to the parish the part my family plays in my life. I told each group that I believed myself to be the most married man in America. I explained that my first and most important ministry was the ministry to my marriage. Then, after explaining the wonderful way in which my wife and I met and married, I asked for their help in this ministry.

"You see," I said, "I am convinced that clergy are not just supposed to talk about family life. I believe we are supposed to live it. I think each of you wants your pastor to have a strong and happy marriage and to be a caring and committed parent. In order to live up to those expectations, I'm going to need your help to pay as much attention to them as I do to you. Here at the beginning of our relationship, I want you to agree with me that the preacher's place is in the home, at least for a significant part of each week. If I start to forget that, you let me know."

The response was warm and sympathetic, and for as long as I served that parish, people came to me and asked, "Are you spending enough time at home?" How I rejoiced in hearing those words!

Planting Symbols

Another key for me has been to establish a visible reminder of my growing relationship with the congregation.

In each parish I have served, I have planted a tree as a sign of our beginning. I have also thought of planting a thousand daffodil or tulip bulbs, and have imagined the glorious blanket of color they would provide the church grounds. But for some reason I have always come back to a flowering tree.

So one Sunday my congregation and I walked out of our morning service and gathered around a young dogwood waiting to be planted.

"I don't have anything fancy to say, just a prayer that this tree — a sign of our beginning a new work together — will bloom for many years, and that even after I'm gone, you will think of this time, as I will, with grateful hearts."

Everyone who could see over heads and shoulders laughed as my clean black shoe was covered by mud as I stamped the root ball deep into the watered hole.

Then, as each spring season arrived, the new growth on the tree and the beauty of its flower was a joyful sign I had been planted in a new home and was rooted there. The planting ceremony itself is a powerful moment and becomes one of the events of parish life that is shared for years to come.

Postpone Your Homecoming

At first it seemed unfortunate that my installation as rector could not take place for eight months following my arrival. The bishop's schedule was booked solid. The vestry felt some frustration and even expressed some of those "we-they" opinions about Episcopal dioceses in general and bishops in particular. Still, we reasoned, we would have plenty of time to prepare for the service, and we could give it a little thought.

We appointed a committee to plan the service and celebration to follow, and they promptly forgot their charge until I called the chairperson six weeks before the scheduled date.

Three weeks later, having heard nothing from the group, I called again.

"Oh, wait until you see what we have lined up for you. Do you know the symbols of office that we are suppose to present during the service? And the congregational response to the letter of institution? Well, all I'll tell you is this: you're going to love it."

And love it I did! The worship service reflected a relationship between pastor and people that had already had time to grow. There were moments of humor and poignancy that were possible only because we had come to know each other over the course of that eight-month period. The celebration included my favorite music, their special food, and a wonderful gift that was acquired not in anonymous haste but with deliberate care.

Whatever the service might have been at my arrival, it was a thousand times better having waited until we were both at home.

Home Is Where the Thought Is

When the children of Israel were in bondage in Babylon, Jeremiah wrote to help ease the pain of exile. His advice seemed deceptively simple: "Build houses, settle down; plant gardens and eat what they produce. . . . Work for the good of the city to which I have exiled you; pray to God on its behalf, since on its welfare yours depends" (Jer. 29:5, 7, NJB). Even outside of exile, Jeremiah's advice is sound: work makes home.

Specifically, the work I invest in the preparation for my arrival, in the house in which I dwell, in friendships planted and nurtured, and in my commitment to my new community bring a sense of home quickly and bring it well.

"Shake the dust off your feet" and move on, Jesus tells his disciples after they are rejected. That is sound advice even in this day. But as we make our way out of town, we will have to traverse some potentially dangerous streets.

— Robert Kemper

CHAPTER SIX

The Forced Termination

We all wish it never happened. Pastors are hurt by it. Congregations suffer for it. The whole body of Christ aches when it happens. But sometimes it happens: a pastor is asked to leave a pastorate. To put it in business terms, sometimes pastors get fired. Like the crash of an airliner, the news is jarring and the effect on people is wide and most unwelcome.

When it happened to Peter Hudson (a composite of fired pastors I've known), he was stunned. It had never occurred to him that anyone as sincere and well meaning as him could be told by a group of parishioners that his services were no longer needed.

So now what does a pastor do? "Shake the dust off your feet" and move on, says Jesus. That is sound advice even in this day. But as we make our way out of town, we will have to traverse some potentially dangerous streets. Often knowing the names and shapes of those streets helps us get safely through them and on to another community of faith.

Be Angry but Do Not Sin

To be dismissed is to be rejected. To be rejected is like being struck a blow. It hurts. The natural, visceral instinct is to hit back, to hurt others as we have been hurt.

For pastors, public recrimination may be the most tempting recourse. We are professionally articulate, and when wounded, we can easily imagine all sorts of ways to verbally assault people or defend ourselves eloquently.

As Peter Hudson packed his books, each pitch of a book into a box punctuated some great defense he was fashioning in his mind. Like Perry Mason, he mentally cross-examined his accusers, demonstrating that every one of their complaints were wrong, shallow, or mean spirited. With the resounding thud of a concordance he heard himself say aloud and with passion, "Ladies and gentlemen of the jury, you must find this defendant innocent on all counts!"

Some pastors, when fired, mount nonverbal assaults on a congregation, resorting to stealing from the church, destroying records, telling secrets.

And never mind how we've counseled people — those getting a divorce, for example — that retaliation gets people nowhere; rejected pastors feel their case is different!

Nonetheless, in our better moments, we recognize that we will find little help or healing in getting back. So this is a difficult street to walk through as we make our way to the next town.

Negotiate the Dismissal

Even if the dismissal is immediate, the pastor will want to

negotiate the terms of severance. Although we may not feel as if we're in a strong bargaining position, a body of custom and law is behind us. The church has accomplished its goal — your dismissal. The price of reaching that goal is subsidized time for you. Take advantage of that time to seek health and healing for yourself.

Use of the parsonage, salary for six months, and benefits for one year (or until next employment) are not uncommon. So pastors will want to keep their heads clear enough to negotiate the maximum severance arrangement and have it put in writing.

In any case, it's wise to negotiate for as much time as possible. To begin with, dismissed pastors have to find a new position, and those who've gone through the process recommend going slowly — lest they repeat the same mistakes they made in choosing the previous parish.

In addition, hurt and anger take time to heal. Before moving into a new position, those emotions must be dealt with.

A Family Affair

Dismissed pastors soon realize they aren't the only ones being "fired." There is also the pastor's family. They are not being fired technically, but they feel the pain nearly as keenly. In addition to feeling victims to the pastor's sudden career change, they also feel vulnerable to the whims of a congregation.

Certainly pastors can expect some support and help from their immediate family, but the care must flow the other way, as well. The family members do not see themselves as vocational counselors; it's not a role they bargained for. So they'll be of limited help in that regard. In addition, they have their own hurts and angers that need attention, some of which must come from the pastor.

In any case, healing family pain will take time and patient effort, as Peter Hudson realized one evening soon after his dismissal. The atmosphere in the home had been tense. During one dinner, Peter's wife, Emily, handed him a bowl of soup, but the bowl was hotter than he had anticipated. It dropped through his fingers. The bowl, a special memento from Emily's family, shattered on the floor with a loud crash.

Emily and Peter just looked at each other, wondering what else could happen. Immediately their 10-year-old, Joanna, dashed from the room, as if to avoid the approaching storm.

But she soon returned with her tube of Super Glue. She told her parents to pick up the pieces. They were going to have to put them together again. It occurred to Peter that such was the task in regard to him, his family, and their future together.

Shame on Me

Another street to traverse is shame. Public rejection, even if unjustified, produces shame in the rejected. And shame is more invasive and corrosive than guilt. We acknowledge the destructive presence of guilt but rarely acknowledge the wages of shame. Yet shame seems more primal: Adam and Eve hid from God not from guilt but from shame.

Shame is powerful because it's directly related to one's self-image. We have high expectations of ourselves, of how we should be treated and understood. To lose one's job is to be judged a failure. To lose one's work is to sense a loss of identity, status, and social relationships.

Like Adam and Eve, then, we want to hide when made ashamed. Some hide literally, not showing their faces in public. Other hide figuratively, not showing their souls even to themselves.

Peter Hudson had little acquaintance with shame, so little in fact, he did not recognize it in himself. He felt inadequate, misplaced, and embarrassed for himself and his family. He slumped when he walked. He looked at no one in the eye. He laughed little.

The outward and visible signs of shame recede when the inner spirit recovers its strength and power. Holding one's head up and looking another in the eye is not just a function of the skeletal system, but of the human spirit.

Recovery from shame happens in two ways. First, we recover a realistic perception of what has happened. The fact is, we're never as totally benighted as shame seems to make us. Second, we allow a sense of grace slowly to grow anew within again.

Vocational Doubt

An old sermon illustration goes like this: A farmer in his field saw a vision one day; in the sky, he read the letters *GPC*. *What did it mean?* he wondered. He concluded he was being told, "Go Preach Christ."

So he left the farm and went into ministry. It was a disaster. Three times he tried and three times he failed at pastoring a church. After his third failure he poured out his story to a wise colleague who said, "You fool! *GPC* meant *Go Plant Corn!*"

So he did, and both God and the farmer were satisfied.

Fired pastors immediately wonder if they were mistaken about that sense of call they felt long ago, a call they were so sure about at the time.

Not everyone can or should be a minister, of course. We have a difficult calling. Not everyone has the gifts necessary to pastor a church. And, frankly, sometimes a dismissal is a sign of that.

But not necessarily. Certainly deciding such an issue at the time of dismissal is not a wise course. We are too vulnerable then.

George Will, in his book *Men at Work*, quotes Hall of Fame pitcher Warren Spahn: "Baseball is a game of failure. Even the best batters fail about 65 percent of the time." George Will adds that no other vocation so remorselessly looks at the performance of its participants, publicly listing daily the box scores of each game.

Well, Mr. Will has not studied the pastorate. For pastors are rigorously judged every week by congregations. And when congregations judge them harshly, pastors judge themselves more harshly still.

But like baseball players, pastors are wise not to decide their career while in the middle of a slump, or worse, when they've been benched. Better to first ask why we're in a slump and what can we do to get out of it.

Often pastors find it helpful to begin by figuring out exactly why they've been dismissed. Often congregations are vague about why they're letting a pastor go: "We just weren't a good match," they say. And sometimes they're simply mistaken as to what went wrong.

Often pastors discover there has been confusion about what the rules of the game were. The congregation was anxious for a preacher, the pastor was an administrator. The congregation wanted a minister in the community, the pastor wanted to shepherd souls.

Because of the intensity of their emotions, many pastors find it helpful to consult a colleague or trusted member of the congregation to help them make this analysis. But it is important that they do so. It often puts the cosmic soul searching about divine vocation into a manageable light.

Back to the Future

A final street to traverse is making plans for the next parish, more specifically, restructuring one's ministry to make the next position more successful. This restructuring, of course, will be based on the analysis made above.

To see the Rev. Dr. Peter Hudson today you would never know he was once fired by a congregation. He is much loved and respected. Only he knows that his present status is the result of having learned that he had special skills but not all skills, that he is good at some things, and not all things. To his amazement and gratitude, he has discovered there are churches that desperately need what he has to offer.

At a minimum, the pastor will approach the next pastorate with a deeper humility and a greater awareness of the complexity of pastoral life. After such an analysis and new plan for ministry, the pastor will also approach the next position with more hope as well.

Shaking the dust off our feet and moving on to another community, then, is a long process. The streets we traverse are potentially dangerous, but with prayer, patience, and the help of loved ones, it can be traversed, and ministry can be renewed.

PART THREE

Building a Ministry

Beginning a new pastorate means first establishing a relationship in which trust can grow. Doing so will benefit each partner for more than the first months, but for years to come.

—Robert Kemper

CHAPTER SEVEN
The First Year

Protestant clergy follow what John Wesley called "an itinerant tradition." We change pastorates often. Clergy and parishes come to many endings and consequently many beginnings. But just because the process of changing leaders is commonplace, it doesn't mean it's uniform or easy.

I've made this transition three times during my ministry. I've discovered that old opinion — that the first year is critical — is correct. How I handle that first year makes a huge difference in the rest of my stay at a church. Having been through three first years,

I've learned a few things.

The Goal: Building Mutual Trust

I've found that the essential factor in enduring, mutually satisfying pastor-parish relationships is trust. More particularly, the congregation and pastor need to allow each other to fulfill specialized roles, to respect each other's status, responsibilities, and privileges.

To use Paul's imagery, there are different parts in the body. An eye does not do what a kidney does. Healthy bodies of Christ are those in which the various parts function both autonomously and symbiotically, where people respect the gifts of others and contribute themselves to the good of the whole.

One minister arrived in his new parish well-qualified and well-meaning, but his previous ministry had been that of a military chaplain. So by instinct, the new minister "took command" of the new parish. From his office came directives on everything from finance to faith. However, the congregation was not a battalion, and quickly came hostile to him. He did not trust them; they did not trust him. He was "relieved of command" in less than a year.

Most congregations are trustworthy. The evidence is on their side; namely, they have existed as a church before the new leader came. They have a good sense of what sustains a Christian community. They understand financial needs, mission initiatives, ecclesiastical purpose. By and large, they are highly idealistic and want to do good. There are no purposefully and willfully malevolent congregations.

On the other hand, most pastors are trustworthy. They have been called of God to ministry; they have been prepared for and have experience in ministry.

So, ministers and congregations are usually trustworthy. The problem is that new congregations and new pastors do not know each other. They have had no experiences that solidify the commitment to each other. They have not met a crisis.

It is not surprising that the metaphor for pastor-parish relations is marriage. A "honeymoon" is the time immediately after the vows have been spoken. In pastor-parish relationships, as in marriage, there is nothing like the relentless pressures of intimacy to disclose the unknown mysteries of another.

Hence, beginning a new pastorate means first establishing a relationship in which trust can grow. Doing so will benefit each partner for more than the first months, but for years to come.

I have known pastors who have done what seemed to me terribly bizarre things in a congregation. But when I asked them how they got away with such things, they inevitably explain that the congregation understands. "That's who I am and how I do things," they say. The Scripture is right when it says there are no strangers and sojourners in the house of the Lord. That's especially true when strangers take the time and effort to become trusted persons in the house.

Trust is, of course, an intangible goal. But I've found a few tangible ways to build it.

Moratorium on Change

When I arrive in a new church, I'm bursting to jump into leadership. But I check my enthusiasm. In fact, I try to make no changes in the church for one year. Instead, I use the first year to wait, listen, and learn. Only then do I lead.

The first year is the only year, of course, when some changes can be made. Maybe the organist has to go before he becomes entrenched in my term. Nonetheless, I've always been cautious about assuming I've been given carte blanche in that first year.

This biding of time is hard on me, however. I'm taken with the old adage, "A new broom sweeps clean." Then again, the hand that guides the broom needs to know where to sweep. My newcomer's hand doesn't know that.

Often, this impatience gets planted in the call process. A congregation looks at its needs and identifies a pastor who can address those needs. That's a set-up: "The new minister will solve our problems." But I remain cautious. A problem usually has a history. If it could have been fixed, it would have been fixed long ago.

For example, let's say the new congregation is divided over

the hour of Sunday morning worship. The divided community says, "We will let the new minister decide what is the right time." Since I do not want to lose half the community, I won't decide the question. Instead, I tell them, "Say what time you want me to be there, and I will be there!"

In addition, quick decisions about intractable problems will probably make me look impetuous, arbitrary, and easily swayed. That is not the way to build trust.

Instead, I wait and listen, especially at the beginning. An anthropologist told me her graduate students learn the most about a new culture in their first fifteen minutes in it. Soon they become acclimatized and start seeing the world as the culture sees it.

So during the first year, while I'm freshly exposed to a new church culture, I actively take mental, and some literal, notes on the congregation. I've always found this type of listening a highly active process for me. I try to be present at everything; I skip nothing. I need to be seen much more than heard, partly because I don't want to stick my foot in my mouth more than necessary!

In particular I ask: *How are children treated--are they seen but not heard? How is money handled--do people always gripe, or is it never mentioned? Is the stranger made welcome here--do people personally take you over to the coffee hour and introduce you to others? Are families interrelated here--is this a literal or symbolic extended family? Is the building something of an icon to this church--do they revere its original design so much that any thought of change would be unthinkable to them?*

Every congregation has a myriad of silent symbols. I need to learn these before I can lead. So I take notes, both appreciative and critical, on what I observe, and I keep them private.

These notes come in handy at the end of my first year. In exchange for not making changes for a year, I often ask the congregation to agree to receive a series of recommendations about their church after that first year. Because my recommendations are based on careful observation, and because a year's worth of trust has been built, these recommendations are usually not only warmly received but create lasting changes.

Leadership is at least a two-legged creature. One leg steps out to where we ought to be going — the future. The other leg is rooted in where we are — the present. Some new ministers fall not because they have no vision, but because they have not gotten their balance where they are. The successful day-care program I inaugurated in First Church may be a disaster in St. Mark's. The success or failure has nothing to do with you or the program; it has to do with first knowing the territory.

Introduction from the Pulpit

Most pastoral search committees want their minister first and foremost to preach effectively. Preaching is the one ministerial skill visible and accessible to the *whole* community. Thus, preaching is a key instrument in the first year of a pastorate.

That corresponds with the new minister's desires, as well. When I'm new to a parish, I am eager to step into the pulpit. I'm also ready to redeliver my best sermons. However, I have always resisted both temptations.

In fact, if it is at all possible, before I ever preach, I try to worship first in the pews of the sanctuary. I may never have another chance to do that. As I sit, I notice how the service sounds from the pew, and I ask myself such questions as *Where should I stand when I preach? Is there a microphone? and What happens when the speaker turns away from it?*

I *think* I know such things because I have done them all before. But I have not done them in *this* place. So I familiarize myself with the unique setting of this congregation.

Soon enough I get to step into the pulpit. What do I say? Knowing that the community wants to become familiar with me, I preach so they can. For instance, I've begun by preaching a series of sermons on basic beliefs. That way the congregation and I will start speaking a common church vocabulary.

Further, I try not to use illustrations from my previous pastorate, not even illustrations that meant a lot to my former parishioners. This is a new community; I cannot count on them understanding as did my previous church. Besides, I want to start building illustrations that connect me with this congregation.

Getting to Know You

Preaching, in which people see me only in my "game uniform," is only one part of getting acquainted. I also want them to know the person who wears the symbols of ministry. And I want to get to know them; that's part of the fun of the first year in a new pastorate. I use four methods to accomplish that end.

● *Write a booklet.* For me, becoming acquainted involves teaching a congregation how to relate to a minister in general and me in particular. So even before arriving, I send my new congregation a small booklet about me and my concept of ministry. I tell them how honored I am to have been invited to become their new pastor. I describe how I became a minister, my credentials, and people and experiences that have influenced me.

I also tell them how to use me — what I like to do best and what I am good at. I tell them the day of the week I will be off. (I also point out that clergy work most when other people are at leisure: evenings, weekends, and holidays. Many are amazed to discover this simple truth.)

If they want me to know something, I ask them to tell me, not my wife. I explain my wife is not responsible for my schedule or my data bank. I tell them if they want to discuss church matters to call me at the church office, not at home. I point out how the church goes to considerable expense to have an office, a secretary, file cabinets, and a telephone at church for me to conduct church business there.

Since all this can be phrased tactfully, my booklet is well-received. My new parishioners not only get to know more of who I am but also how I want to be treated.

● *Invite them over.* Since I have an agreeable spouse, and since I've always enjoyed a lifestyle compatible with my congregations, I usually invite the entire congregation into my home in groups of twenty or so for an "Evening with the Pastor." I keep it informal, maybe dessert and coffee, and simply have people mingle during the first part.

Then I invite the group to assemble, and I ask them each to

offer their personal story, suggesting an outline to follow. I ask them to conclude by telling us about their fondest hope for our church. I am continually surprised at what I learn in this setting. And it's guaranteed — next Sunday I will see them in church!

I've structured these social gatherings in a variety of ways. For instance, I've had afternoon teas for all who have been members for more than fifty years, cookouts for the youth group, and evenings with young families. Since I am still learning who is who, the board of deacons has helped me arrange invitations so the whole congregation is included.

In any case, having people into my home is a significant symbol. If the home is a parsonage, members need to see their own property. (Once, after doing this in a parsonage, there was a great rush to find a more "suitable" home for the minister!) Also, my home says something about my tastes, which say something about who I am.

• *See them at work.* If it's possible, I try to visit my parishioners at their places of employment. First, however, I ask them to invite me to do so.

Although most don't take me up on the invitation, many do. So I've had wonderful afternoons in factories, schools, offices, and airports. I often learn more about my parishioners in one visit than I could seeing them in church for a year. In addition, I've begun to identify with them and their concerns.

• *Celebrate!* The coming of a new minister is a festive moment for a congregation. They are glad to see us and want to welcome us into their community. It is an excuse for a party, and I've had no qualms about exploiting that festive spirit.

My denomination has a ritual for the installation of a new minister, but I've never felt like rushing the installation service. I don't even mind waiting six months after I arrive if that gives us additional time to plan some festive moments for the church.

If music is the congregation's forte, I invite the choirs and organist to plan an installation week music festival. I also invite the whole community for this spectacular event. Or we might have an art show, inviting local artists to present their works. Or we might have a picnic in a nearby public park, or a softball, golf, or horseshoe tournament. Most anything will do to celebrate the presence of a new minister!

In addition, a variety of supporting events can be added. I have twice invited local clergy to a special lecture given by a recognized religious leader. They listened to this visiting dignitary, had lunch, welcomed me, and went on about their day glad that a new colleague had come among them.

Special groups in the congregation need special welcoming parties. I have had ice cream and cake on the lawn with school-age children, rocked through a teenage dance, potlucked with seniors, and sat through sporting events with sports fans. All this frivolity in the name of welcoming a new pastor! The church became a place where everyone was welcomed and people enjoyed being together. Not a bad definition of community.

In pastoral work, most mistakes can be corrected. Not so with beginnings; I cannot begin at a congregation twice. So I'm especially urgent about using this unique opportunity well. If thoughtfully and imaginatively done, the events of the first year set a tone and approach that a pastor and congregation can enjoy for years to come.

As I've moved into parishes and become acquainted with people, especially as I've begun to plan for that congregation's future, I've found it especially important to know and appreciate the congregation's past.

— Doug Scott

CHAPTER EIGHT

Harnessing Your Church's History

The history of a congregation is no more real to most church members than a list of names were to the little girl in the old joke. She saw the names of military personnel on a bronze memorial plaque and asked her mother, "Who are all those people?"

"Why, they are members of our church who died in the service," the mother replied.

"Which one," asked the daughter, "8:00 or 10:30?"

We may briefly study the history of our faith and perhaps the life of a denomination, but for many members, a church's history amounts to who ran last year's church fair. For others, it's the last congregational crisis, which they would just as soon forget. For some, history is the row of dusty board minutes squashed in stationery-store binders on a neglected shelf, or a list of faceless clergy, or the old crank who complains, "We never *used* to do it this way!" For others still, history is nostalgia for the old *Book of Common Prayer* or the King James Version.

That's too bad, because a congregation's history is rich with meaning. As I've moved into parishes and become acquainted with the people, especially as I've begun to plan for that congregation's future, I've found it especially important to know and appreciate the congregation's past.

History Shows God at Work Here

A few months ago, our congregation was pressed by a few extraordinary expenses. Since we faced a summer of low attendance and even lower offerings, many were inclined to doubt that God was active here and now. So I announced that next week I would preach the most important sermon since my arrival: "Where Is God Today?"

The following week, I stood in the pulpit and reviewed *recent* church history: "In the last two years, people from this congregation have served an evening meal twice a week to homeless men and women at St. Barnabas Shelter. Members of this church have made forty-five hospital calls on the sick and sixty calls on shut-ins. Six people, taught by members of this church, are learning how to read. You have provided the equivalent of nine hundred meals for our area food cupboard. Five of you drive for Meals on Wheels; eight of you volunteer in our hospital and area nursing homes; one volunteers in the state prison.

"Since I have served here, more than $40,000 has gone out of this parish to help build a school in Uganda, provide livestock for hungry farmers around the world, buy blankets for refugees, and provide disaster relief. Another $65,000 has supported our home missions. That's where God is today."

The pastor who helps the people explore their own activity in the recent past allows them to see the movement of God in their common life.

History Creates Community

During one Lenten group discussion, a woman blurted out to her neighbor, "We were wrong!" Naturally, everyone turned toward her. Realizing she had drawn the attention of the room, she said, "I was just talking about something that happened more than twenty years ago. At the time, we had a young assistant who was strongly opposed to the Vietnam War. It seemed that every sermon was about Vietnam and every news broadcast carried film of him being arrested in a protest. We fought him tooth and nail until he left in despair. But we were wrong."

Several people started talking, but she spoke over them. "I don't mean his political position was right or wrong. I mean the way we acted toward him was wrong. We rejected him because he held an unpopular position, and we never stopped to ask whether God was trying to say something to us through his ministry."

One of our newest members broke in and talked about a similar experience in the church he attended at the time. Another, born at the end of the Vietnam era, asked questions, trying to recapture the urgency of the times.

By the end of the evening, the group was talking together about *our* history and *their* histories. The living memory of the congregation became real and powerful. By the time the session ended, we each felt we had a share in the church. Now, in each gathering of newcomers, we incorporate a time when we talk about our experience in the congregation. We invite our new members to share something of their history and that of their churches. We find such sharing binds us together.

I imagine the early church must have talked in this way. Christians who met each other on the road no doubt excitedly shared the story of what the Spirit had been doing in their communities, naming those who had been healed or lifted up, remembering things all the way back to the time when they first heard Christ's story.

History Shapes a Church's Future

For good or ill, a church's history influences its future attitudes or action. This can go far beyond the usually well-broadcast
theological or liturgical stance of many congregations — liberal or
conservative, high or low, evangelical or charismatic.

I had served a congregation for more than a year and a half,
and after a shorter-than-usual honeymoon, I kept running into
resistance. There weren't any grave doctrinal or ideological differences between us, just a relentless opposing force, its edges soft-
ened by a steady stream of smiles and politeness. I couldn't get
anything done.

Finally, I asked a few board members to sit down with me for
an informal conversation. "Do you get a sense that there's an objec-
tion to almost everything I propose?" They looked at each other
with some confusion. "There seems to be some polite verbal resistance to any idea I suggest. I've even encountered it when I've
suggested that we continue with the status quo!"

They agreed with my perception but didn't consider it particularly unusual. "Do you mean this kind of resistance is standard
operating procedure around here?" I asked. They assured me, in a
matter-of-fact way, that was the way the board operated. I was
astonished.

"But what about my predecessors? Did they each face this
kind of pleasant negativity?" Yes, they supposed that was probably
the case.

I then asked them to fill me in on the histories of the men who
had preceded me in that church. When they were finished, I was
both amazed and frightened. They had shared a tragic litany of
short tenures, divorce, and addictive and self-destructive behavior.

After more research, I discovered that many of the clergy who
had served that congregation absorbed their anxiety about the parish, to the detriment of their own physical or spiritual well-being.
No simple conclusions can be drawn from the complex history of
forty years of ministry. But I did see that my own behavior eventually could have placed me on the church's honor role of martyred

clergy. That prospect disturbed me.

While I knew the essential dates and events in the church's life, I knew very little about the *real* history of the parish — the one written in the emotions and attitudes of its people.

Learning the Real History

Since I believe such knowledge is vital for a successful ministry, my wife and I sat down with a parish list and a two-year calendar. We divided the church into groups small enough to host at our home, and we have planned dinner parties for them according to these simple principles:

1. We invite no more than six other people to these dinners, which are held once a month. That makes it easier on our budget.

2. We mix relative newcomers with longstanding members.

3. We gather on Sunday nights. If people know they are going to face me at my dinner table, they tend to be in worship that morning.

4. Only one disgruntled couple is invited per night. And when we have invited an unhappy twosome, we also have invited some of our most enthusiastic supporters to sit with them.

5. No matter what food we serve, the story is always the main dish. Our guests may digress into football and television (and I happily sojourn with them for a while). But I want us to talk primarily about issues and events of past congregational life. If I have heard the stories before, I want our guests' reaction to them. I never pass judgment, instruct, or persuade. I ask questions and listen.

I begin by asking questions about the one subject most people are eager to discuss — their children.

Did your children enjoy their Sunday school experience?

What did they find most memorable?

Did their Sunday school/early worship experience prepare them adequately for Christian living?

Is there anything that should have received greater emphasis?

Were they baptized/married here? What was the service like?

If my guests have moved from another congregation or denomination within the last ten years, I also ask them:

What factors drew you to this church?

Was it difficult to adjust from your former congregation? Why?

What made the transition easy? Would anything have made it easier?

I tell my guests I am fascinated by stories about the church and I wish I knew more. Usually, people are glad to dig around for something interesting to tell, especially if I prompt them:

What do you think has been the most important event in the life of the church since you have been a member? In many respects, their *perception* of important events is far more important than the historical value of the events themselves.

Tell me about my predecessor's strong points. What do you miss most about his ministry here?

I always honor my predecessor, even if he left in absolute disgrace. Most people hold some measure of affection for their former pastor and appreciate an opportunity to share their feelings, especially if they see I am not threatened by their care for him. In an open atmosphere, they likely will speak as well about the shortcomings of previous ministries, even though I have been wise enough not to ask.

Have you ever been tempted to leave this church? What prompted the feeling? Why did you decide to stay? Everyone thinks about leaving at some point. If discretion permits, I try to share with them the times I have thought about leaving and the reasons. One of the strongest things I have in common with members is the fact that we both have decided to stay.

What has been the single biggest change in twenty years? In some denominations, like my own, you can predict the answer: change in form of worship, authority, or doctrinal stance. However, people's reactions to that change may not be so predictable. While some of our members feel that reasonable change is the moral responsibility of the church, others find it a betrayal of a long-held trust. Again, my concern is not the issue itself but their response to it. I wanted to focus on the key issue: Have you been able to sense God at work in the life of this congregation?

In the last year alone, my wife and I have fed over 110 members of our church at our table. We, in turn, have been served a banquet of invaluable richness of our church's past. Our guests have seen God at work where they didn't see him before, have drawn closer to one another, and have been given new hope for the church's future.

Thwarting the History that Steals Hope

If history can provide hope, it also can steal hope. Scripture is filled with examples of people who held on to the past to keep people from moving forward. The children of Israel, unable to share Moses' vision, began to see their slavery in Egypt as the good old days. The circumcision party in Jerusalem was unable to grasp the radical new inclusiveness of the Way. The story has been the same throughout the history of Christianity. Just look at the minutes of any church board.

We should honor honest caution and sober reflection. But fear frequently compels a conscientious steward to let past failure dictate future policy. Pastors can transform the obsession with past failures into hope, especially if they draw the people back to their history and common ministry.

Whenever any group has been held up by the thievery of history, I ask them to go through a simple process. Stating that I deeply value the lessons of our common past, I ask them to consider three questions. We take plenty of time for the exercise. That demonstrates how much we respect the concern that surrounds the issue. The three questions, taken in turn, are:

1. Are there historical corollaries in the life of this congregation that relate to our current situation? How about in the life of our denomination? In our families?

2. Are we looking at the *right* history to illuminate this situation? What other historical events might also parallel this situation?

3. What new things in this situation change our perceptions of history or render history irrelevant?

My congregation recently used this procedure when looking

at the all-too-common problem of rapidly rising expenses versus moderately rising income. For over a year, our vestry struggled with possible cuts in personnel and program to bring expenses in line with income. Finally, we admitted we were of two minds — the You-can't-squeeze-blood-from-a-stone Party and the Just-send-each-household-a-bill Party.

We set aside an entire evening to explore the three questions listed above. In order to secure the integrity of the exercise, I announced that we wouldn't even consider possible approaches to the problem at this stage.

Discussion following the first question revealed that the congregation, in fact, had faced substantial deficits in the past. These deficits were due to a variety of factors, including inflation, extraordinary capital expenses, and parish disputes. In addition, we identified times when some members created a budget crisis by withholding pledges in order to influence vestry policy.

The identification of other times when the church faced — and survived — a budget shortfall immediately gave the group confidence. They also recognized that money and crisis are constant companions in the church, and that they need not blame themselves for the exigencies of parish finance.

One vestry member said later, "I realized for the first time that my charge to do the best I can with parish resources did not mean I was expected to provide another loaves-and-fishes miracle."

The second question forced us to examine our situation critically. This was not a case of withheld tithes by angry members or irresponsible vestry spending. We were faced with the overwhelming costs of periodic maintenance for our ten-acre campus and its two-hundred-year-old buildings. Paint peels, and slate roofs eventually crumble.

We also saw that time and again, when the congregation felt their church property was threatened or endangered, they had responded quickly and generously. Had we looked at the wrong piece of history — one not similar to our current crisis — our response would have been misguided and ill-informed.

The third question allowed us to identify a new factor in our situation. In recent years, our outreach and mission ministries had grown dramatically. Our congregation had practiced outreach with vigor; new people were being drawn in because of our efforts on behalf of others. But so far, we had worked only for other churches' programs; there was no indigenous mission springing from our church. We realized that we had the interest and talent to take on a mission project, and that we might have the goodwill to finance it, as well.

In the end, this process allowed us to see that, instead of being at the point of collapse, we were at a moment of tremendous opportunity to restore the property and begin a great work. Our deliberations resulted in a major capital campaign that drew to a successful close. A group of church members then met to research opportunities for mission, and the restoration of our buildings got underway. And enough money was raised to begin an endowment that will insure future money for ministry.

In short, we used history to take back what history started to steal.

History: The Tie that Binds

On the best days when I worship with my people, I grasp in a fresh way that I am not alone. Certainly, I am in a room filled with people. But beyond that, I am exquisitely aware of the presence of others unseen, worshiping with us. The author of the Epistle to the Hebrews wrote about us being "surrounded by so great a cloud of witnesses." That's how I feel at those moments. When we stand at the Lord's Table, I get a glimpse of the many faithful people who have stood there, breaking bread and sharing the cup in their own generations.

At such times I also realize anew that the greatest things do not only bring our history forward and make it present to us, but they also point us toward the future.

Our Communion with Christ is not just the reenactment of something finished, but also an act that has brought us together in the present and directs us toward a common goal.

When we read Scripture, we read not only the Word of God

for the prophets and evangelists, but also the Word of God *for us*, confident that it will be the Word of God for our children and their children after them.

The hymns we sing, whether written in the ninth or nineteenth century, bring the praise of faithful men and women to our own lips, and their words and melodies carry us through the week, giving voice to our praise and planting hope in our despair.

Worship, then, shows us that if we ignore history, we not only build our ministries on sand, we also ignore the Lord who created, lived in, and continues to use history to strengthen us. No, history is not something dead and gone. It is something that helps us make sense of the present and hope for the future, especially as we enter a new congregation. In short, knowing the congregation's history can give today's ministry a foundation that will stand the test of time.

Each of us is somebody's predecessor — that truth helps me understand better the relationship I should have with my predecessor.

— Robert Kemper

The Shadow of Your Predecessor

You'd been familiar with the fine reputation of Old First Church for some time, so when Dr. Adams resigned from it you thought maybe, just maybe, this was what God had been preparing you for. Old First had been served by only three senior ministers in the last fifty years; Dr. Adams, himself, accounted for twenty of those years. He retired almost a year ago at age 67. And now you have the chance to join the procession of distinguished pastors in this great church.

After submitting your dossier, you were delighted to hear that your name came to the attention of the pastoral search committee. They thought you met their profile, so they invited you for a conversation. That led to an invitation to preach.

Soon the initiative shifted; they began wooing you. Eventually you emerged as the committee's selection to be the next senior minister at Old First Church. What a great moment for you!

You preach your first sermon, and all goes well. You make your way to the church's cavernous fellowship hall where a reception for you and your family awaits. As you greet your new congregation in a receiving line, you notice off to the side that a sizable and growing knot of people is forming in one corner. When you finish greeting people, you amble over. You soon see that the crowd is gathered around a distinguished-looking, gray-haired, freshly-tanned gentleman, just back from a ten-month interim pastorate in Sun City.

A member of the pastoral search committee grabs you by the arm and whisks you through the crowd. "I want you to meet Charley," he beams. Charles Adams finishes patting a parishioner on the back and turns toward you. His big hand goes out in practiced greeting. "Hello, young man, welcome to First Church!"

This scene may be exaggerated, but in some new pastorates, we feel like the predecessor is with us from day one. He may have left physically, but his spirit sits at our desk, stands in our pulpit, and roams our halls.

This is to be expected, especially if the previous pastor had a significant ministry in the church. We all hope our ministries will continue to impact congregations after we're gone. The predecessor becomes a problem, however, when his memory interferes with the ministry of the new pastor.

Then again, some predecessors never physically leave the parish — or they return shortly after retirement. This becomes troublesome when they continue to minister to the congregation despite their resignation. Closely related are predecessors who, although not physically present, still keep their hand in the business of the church: they still have loyalists who faithfully report to them and through whom they regularly communicate the predecessor's will for the congregation.

Each of these manifestations of a predecessor presents a unique challenge. Each requires a unique strategy.

Dealing with the Memory

In dealing with the absent but fondly remembered pastor, I've found it helpful to remember four things.

● *A strong memory may mean a strong future.* It's likely that a predecessor has a firm hold on the congregation's memory because he or she maintained a solid ministry for a long time. Three times in three very different settings I followed such long-term pastors, and each time with good results.

Long pastorates usually signal that a congregation is stable and has a strong sense of identity. It also shows that a congregation has the ability to remain faithful over the long run. And that only bodes well for my ministry. So I'm happy to live with the inconvenience of a powerful congregational memory of a predecessor.

● *Congregational memory is selective.* When we step into a new pastorate, we're newcomers. We know our predecessors only as they are now in the memory of the congregation, not as they were then in the presence of the congregation. Churches tend to forget thorns and remember blossoms; so parishioners often revere only part of what was — the good part. And the more the months and years pass, the more selective is the congregation's perception of the predecessor.

It may be that Dr. Adams wore out five years ago and coasted downhill toward his long overdue retirement. It may be that he was a sloppy administrator, or perhaps he never gave attention to children and youth. But we hear only about his fine preaching or his exemplary community involvement.

If we're not careful, we may begin competing with Dr. Adams and pursue ministries that don't fit us. Or we may try to outdo Dr. Adams all together. But we'll be trying to outdo superpastor, not the real person who ministered. It's good to realize we live with second-hand images of the past. We mustn't take them too literally.

● *The predecessor did some good.* I assume God called my predecessor to the church and used him or her to minister to people. So, I always honor and speak well of my predecessor. Besides, any criticism of predecessors reflects finally on me.

If I come upon repugnant practices undertaken by my predecessor, I tell only a ministerial colleague. I find a pastoral friend to whom I can speak freely about my frustration, knowing that my friend will listen to my complaint with understanding and compassion.

● *I am somebody's predecessor.* When I take the trouble to picture life for my successor, I notice that nobody wins. If my successor comes and ruins everything, I will despise the successor for undoing what I spent years to create. Then again, if my successor does well, it will look as if I've been "dogging" it or simply ineffective all these years.

Each of us is somebody's predecessor — that truth helps me understand better the relationship I should have with my predecessor. Mostly, it makes me more humble about my situation. When I tire of hearing about the greatness of my predecessor, I remember that the congregation's memory of me will irritate my successor. When I'm tempted to judge my predecessor, I remind myself that we have different gifts. In addition, we minister in unique circumstances — even when we serve the same congregation. The wonders of pastor So-and-so in the 1950s have no relationship to the wonders I hope to accomplish in the 1990s.

Dealing with a Present Predecessor

Sometimes a predecessor remains in the community and, worse, in the congregation. That fact is likely to cause a measure of panic in the pastor; it seems to be a guaranteed formula for disaster. But all is not lost if certain practices are adhered to.

● *Establish clear ground rules.* My second pastorate was a middle-sized parish in New Jersey. The day the moving van pulled into my driveway to deliver my household goods, my predecessor came to call.

After exchanging pleasantries, he informed me that he intended to live in the community and be a member of the church.

Naturally, I was concerned. But he promised me he would (1) never comment about my ministry to others, (2) do anything in the congregation I did not first ask him to do, and (3) take no public stand on any issue before the congregation.

Admittedly, I was intimidated by and skeptical of this proposition. But this pastor was a man true to his word. To the best of my knowledge he never broke that promise. In fact, I had a friend, a colleague, and a supporter.

In this case, my predecessor approached me. But if he hadn't, I would have soon made a call on him and worked out this or a similar agreement.

• *Make use of the predecessor.* In addition, we can ask the predecessor to perform occasional duties in the church — e.g., calling on shut-ins, teaching an adult class. This not only furthers our ministries, it also enhances the self-esteem of predecessors, calling on their gifts and experience. A predecessor so affirmed is less likely to interfere with the present ministry and, instead, will probably support it.

• *Keep control of the situation.* I always insist that requests to have a former pastor, present or distant, perform a wedding or funeral come through me. No matter how friendly we are with one another or how much I trust the predecessor's judgment, I need to keep clear the lines of accountability. If I'm going to have an effective ministry, people must recognize who the pastor is.

• *When trouble brews, take decisive action.* I've not had this experience, but in talking with pastors who have, four steps emerge.

First, make sure there really is trouble and not just a misinterpretation. What exactly is the predecessor doing? With whom? To what effect? How often?

Next we have to determine how much of this activity we can take. For some pastors, *one* interference is too many. Others excuse episodes and look for patterns.

Third, when our tolerance finally runs thin, we should go to the former pastor and ask him or her to simply cease and desist.

Finally, if that doesn't work, we can go to our parish board, describe the dilemma, and ask them to intervene. Once the former pastor sees that the church officially discourages such activity, he or she will likely stop.

Some denominations have procedures in such instances, and in an extreme case we might have to ask the denomination to intervene.

In the end, we have no choice but to reach out and take Dr. Adams's hand and shake it firmly. Even if he's not physically present, he's going to be present in the minds of the congregation and in the life of the parish. Rather than chafe at his presence, better to learn to work with him.

Preaching and visitation are essential in any pastorate, but in a broken church, their need is magnified. Our members needed to hear the Good News of God's love and power, to have their hope renewed, and to experience human concern and love.

— Ed Bratcher

CHAPTER TEN
Following a Difficult Pastorate

I was jogging down the street, thinking about my new church (I had arrived in Manassas only a few weeks earlier), when a man I had never seen motioned with his hand for me to stop. I stopped and tried to catch my breath.

"Are you the new pastor of Manassas Baptist?" he asked.

"Yes," I said, smiling.

"I'll never go there again!" he exclaimed heatedly. Then he began an angry tirade about the church's hypocrisy, its control by a few members, its lack of love. It took him thirty minutes to finish.

I could tell he had been deeply hurt, but I wasn't sure what to say. I only knew this was going to be the most difficult pastorate of my ministry.

Following a Fallen Pastor

The previous pastor at Manassas, whom I'll call Fred Sharpe, had resigned under pressure from charges of sexual indiscretions and aberrant theology. When I had candidated, the pastoral search committee described the problems in general terms, with a note of sadness. "Fred was a man of unusual abilities," they explained.

Before Fred had become pastor, the congregation had been divided on whether to call him, but Fred had been highly recommended and had demonstrated qualities the congregation sought: he was articulate, personable, and young, and he held a reputation for leading churches into growth.

The church grew rapidly under Fred's ministry. Many were attracted to his nontraditional approach to preaching and worship, and soon a second service was started. After about eighteen months, however, a few people started leaving the church, upset primarily by Fred's theology and his practice of drinking beer in public. There were also rumors of sexual indiscretions.

As I had considered the call to Manassas, Fred was still living in the community and had started a "Church Without Walls." The Manassas Baptist Church staff was in disarray: one of the associate pastors had resigned; the other was having serious marital problems. I sensed the church's financial condition was unstable, even though the interim pastor assured me this was not the case. (Time proved him wrong.)

For these reasons, among others, I struggled for three months with whether to go to Manassas. But I accept as a good definition of God's call "a task to be done and the ability to do it." People told me they felt I had the abilities, so after much prayer, I accepted the call.

Trying to Get the Total Story

I thought I had the full story when I went. But about six months after I arrived, Fred moved in with his girlfriend. Neither was divorced at that time. I learned that Fred's sexual improprieties had been going on for several years and had caused severe strains in his marriage. The search committee had not mentioned the problem; no one knew the extent or severity of it until Fred and his wife separated.

Every member's attitude toward me and the church was in some way colored by these past events, yet each person viewed those events in different ways. It was difficult to get a clear picture of what had happened.

The complexity of the situation can be seen in the different reminiscences of four members:

A strong supporter of Fred: "I'm not sure why I wasn't aware of the moral problems, except that maybe I wasn't in contact with anyone who disagreed with us. Those who agree with an embattled pastor tend to surround him and cut him off from divergent viewpoints. There were a few vague charges brought out at a couple of business meetings, but they were discounted."

A female church leader: "Looking back, I realize Fred was making improper overtures to some of the women. Tales came back to me of such actions taking place at retreats, but they also occurred in the homes of the members."

A deacon who opposed Fred: "My opposition began when Fred preached a sermon on 'Open Marriage,' the essence of which was biblically and morally unsound. Prior to that sermon, I had become concerned about rumors that Fred, in his home, encouraged young people to experiment with alcoholic beverages (though only in moderation)." When this deacon's opposition became vocal, many members reported to him rumors of Fred's sexual indiscretions. He took these rumors seriously because of the people who reported them. "By the time a vote of confidence was called for, I was convinced Fred was involved in extramarital affairs, and that was the major issue in my mind in seeking Fred's resignation."

One of the staff members who worked with Fred: "I was supportive of Fred's program. I also feel the church leaders shielded me from the conflict. I was still in my 20s, so they didn't want me to get hurt in the crossfire. I was concerned over the problems Fred and his wife were having, and as a result, I probably was not 'hearing' what was being said about Fred."

A Plethora of Problems

Fred's sexual behavior was not the only issue in the controversy, but when Fred moved in with his girlfriend, immorality became *the* problem for members of the church. This public confirmation of their suspicions caused the members who were left at Manassas Baptist to forget the other facets of the problem, and therefore made the healing process more difficult.

Among the other problems, for example, was a power struggle between the old and new members. The rapid influx of new members had made the older leadership concerned over their own loss of power. Many leaders had been upset, for instance, the time Fred asked some older members to withdraw their names from consideration as deacons so newer members could be elected. The older members also resented several new programs pushed through by Fred.

At one of the first business meetings I attended, a conflict erupted over whether a nonmember should teach a Sunday school class. The problem was seen as a clash between those who had caused Fred's resignation and those who had supported him. The debate shed little light but generated much heat.

One of the two major adult Sunday school classes had identified itself as "conservative," and the other considered itself "liberal". The "conservative" class saw its task as combating any remaining influences of Fred's theology and lifestyle. The "liberal" class saw its task as combating the rigidness they identified with the opponents of Fred's ministry.

Meanwhile, Fred and his new church were still in the community. He sent a letter to selected members of Manassas Baptist inviting them to the new church he had started. I called him and questioned the ethics of that practice.

"I don't see anything wrong with it," he replied. "I have many friends at Manassas who would like to know what I'm doing. I won't stop contacting those members or any others I might choose."

Fred's behavior plus these conflicts scattered the leadership at Manassas Baptist. A new Baptist congregation had started in town while Fred was still pastor at Manassas Baptist, and, over several months, a number of members saw this as an opportunity to respond to a new challenge (of starting a church) as well as a way out of a difficult situation. In addition, Fred had taken with him many of his followers.

I had the remaining members, many of whom were hurt and disillusioned. Some withdrew from active participation, but the rest became a united remnant committed to praying and working for the rebirth of the congregation.

As a result of these complex and overlapping problems, I learned to accept all reports with a grain of salt. I had to listen with a "third ear" for the feelings and hidden agendas behind each statement.

In many ways I proceeded like Abraham, seeking to follow God's will but not knowing fully where I was going. My age, 50, was a definite asset. Had I been 35 or 40, I doubt if I would have survived. The problems I had gone through in three previous pastorates helped me to listen better and also to retain my hope for a positive resolution.

Leadership Strategies

I began by taking some specific steps to rebuild trust in the pastoral office and unity in the church. Here are the principles that guided me through this challenging new pastorate:

● *Work primarily with and through the board.* Shortly after I arrived at Manassas, I scheduled an overnight retreat with the deacons to deal with whether to keep the two staff members who had survived the conflict. I decided to ask the deacons — rather than the personnel committee — to make the decision. Most of the standing committees were severely weakened by the exodus of trained leaders during the conflict, and therefore, the real power was with the deacons.

I indicated to the deacons that the decision had to be theirs; I was not going to decide for them. One deacon took me aside before the retreat and said, "Ed, the deacons are looking to you for guidance. You must be prepared to share your views." I assured him that I would, but that I wanted the deacons to make the final decision.

The retreat proved exhausting. The first session on Friday evening went until midnight, and many of the deacons continued their discussions until 2 or 3 A.M.

On Saturday morning after prayer time and a devotional, we tested for a consensus. There was none. All of us were emotionally drained and discouraged.

So after sharing with the group what the one deacon and I had talked about, I made three specific recommendations: (1) that both the associate pastor and the part-time minister of music remain, because I needed their help, and it was unfair to dismiss them without notice because of the church's financial problems; (2) that the associate pastor and his wife, recently separated, be given our love and support in this difficult time in their lives; and (3) that the position of the associate pastor be re-evaluated after one year. These provided the catalyst for further discussion, and we decided unanimously to present these recommendations to the church.

Our recommendations were accepted with little discussion by the congregation. This was to be the pattern at the monthly church business meetings for several years to come. The church members were so tired of fighting they wouldn't voice opposition or offer suggestions.

To those familiar with congregational meetings, this might appear to be a godsend! It was only in part. We were left without feedback, so it was hard to develop strategies and programs for which the members had any enthusiasm or sense of ownership.

I continued to use the deacons for several years as the primary, if not the only, decision-making group in the church. By the time I left, however, the deacons were primarily concerned with family ministry and spiritual growth. The various committees — finance, personnel, missions, building and grounds, and others — were again functioning well and carrying out their assignments with minimal input from the deacons.

● *Focus on the pastoral basics, preaching and visitation.* At the first deacons' meeting, I outlined my priorities. First, I would spend the greater portion of my time in visitation; specifically, my wife, Marjie, and I planned to visit each deacon. Second, I would focus on my preaching. I stated also that I would not, for the most part, get involved in rebuilding or strengthening church programs.

Preaching and visitation are essential in any pastorate, but in a broken church, their need is magnified. At Manassas, the members needed to hear the Good News of God's love and power, to have their hope renewed, and to experience human concern and love. These aims were best achieved through preaching and visitation.

A serendipity of my announcement that Marjie and I would be visiting in the homes of deacons was that many invited us for a meal. This provided the double benefit of giving and receiving love.

● *Combat the spirit of failure through constant encouragement.* I'm not by nature a glad-hander and ego builder. I don't make it a practice to announce how great the church is and how wonderful the services have been. My preaching style tends rather to "afflicting the comfortable."

However, four years before going to Manassas, I heard a series of lectures that encouraged pastors to pattern their preaching after Isaiah's words: "Comfort ye, comfort ye my people." At first I rebelled against that suggestion, but at Manassas I turned to it more and more.

Twice, for instance, I preached on Barnabas, "one who encourages," and how he was an example to us. The response was overwhelming; people realized they needed to encourage one another.

To help the church feel it had a viable place in the community, I initiated an annual "Interchurch Conference," to which all the local churches were invited. We brought in major speakers and underwrote the expenses. As the conferences were enthusiastically received by others in the community, people in the church began to feel encouraged that the church was doing something constructive.

I also felt that instilling a spirit of encouragement was also the responsibility of the deacons. I even confronted them once about their discouragement, suggesting that they weren't inviting others to church because they were ashamed of our church. Most agreed I was on target.

• *Help the church to focus outward.* A fourth strategy was to encourage the church to focus on missions. Because my parents were missionaries for forty years, I have a strong commitment to missions. In addition, I found the congregation already had several missions interests I was able to nurture.

We invited missionary couples to the church; one spent a whole week teaching all age groups, including adults, during our Vacation Bible School. Local mission needs were identified as well, and Manassas Baptist took the leadership in providing help to an unexpected influx of refugees. These efforts resulted in a dramatic increase in missions giving, not to mention a renewed sense of congregational purpose.

• *Celebrate the good.* A broken church needs to highlight occasions when it can celebrate the blessings of God. We held services in which we focused on God's goodness in the lives of individuals. We took time to express publicly our thanks for the service of various members and staff.

When our church reached its centennial, we held a year-long celebration with the theme: "Thankful for the past and committed to a second century of ministry." The centennial celebration included historical pageants, the writing of the history of the church, a homecoming Sunday, and a banquet.

Personal Survival Tactics

In pastoring a hurting church, we expend so much that personal survival tactics become as important as leadership strategies, perhaps more so.

My first survival tactic was a redoubling of my efforts in personal spiritual growth. I had been aware for many years that I was often more concerned about leading worship than in participating in it. Marjie gave me a framed copy of a prayer by Martin Luther that so impressed me, I began praying it before every service:

O Lord God, Thou hast made me a pastor and teacher in the church. Thou seest how unfit I am to administer rightly this great, responsible office; and had I been without Thy aid and counsel, I would surely have ruined it long ago. Therefore do I invoke Thee. How gladly do I desire to yield and consecrate my heart and mouth to this ministry. I desire to teach the congregation. I, too, desire ever to learn and to keep Thy Word my constant companion and to meditate thereupon earnestly. Use me as Thy instrument in Thy service. Only do not Thou forsake me, for if I am left to myself, I will certainly bring it all to destruction. Amen.

I asked the deacons to meet with me for prayer prior to the service. Some saw it as a spiritual crutch and resisted the idea at first, but eventually, "prayer with the pastor" became an important part of the role of the deacons.

I found myself spending more and more time in prayer — on prayer retreats, on Saturday evenings in the dark sanctuary. I was not alone in trying to grow spiritually. One member in writing her recollection of the key events over those difficult years concluded by saying, "There is now a solid foundation being built in regard to the spiritual life — prayer, meditation, and Bible study."

A second strategy was to be more open about asking for help from church members. My first major attempt at this came at the time of the marriage of our daughter. She was not known to the church, because she had already established her own career and home before we moved to Manassas. I announced she was to be married in another state and that Marjie would be gone a couple of weeks to help with the wedding preparations. I planned to follow later to perform the ceremony.

I received no response from the congregation. No one seemed to be interested. I had tried to "weep with those who weep, and rejoice with those who rejoice," but now it seemed like those whom I had tried to serve were letting me down. I felt hurt and angry.

While jogging late one evening, I decided to go to one of the families in the church and talk about it. The family listened to me, and they contacted others. By the time I left for the wedding, there was an outpouring of love through various words and deeds.

On the Sunday I returned, I preached on "Carry One Another's Burdens." It was to have been just another sermon, but somehow I was able to confess how hurt I had been, and also how much I had been helped by their love and support. I stood before the members of the church at the time of the altar call and said, "I need you, and I thank you for your love."

Many still speak of that worship hour as one of the highlights of my fifteen-year ministry there. "Carry One Another's Burdens" became something of a motto for many in the congregation.

I also gave attention to the many other sources of renewal available to a pastor. Continuing education events helped me not only because I learned new things about ministry, but also because such classes got me away from the stress of the church. Writing a book, teaching classes, speaking to groups, and consulting were outside interests that I learned to pursue — with the encouragement of the congregation. Both Marjie and I, being duty oriented, had to grow in our ability to allow ourselves to enjoy outside interests. We also began traveling and enjoyed it immensely.

Prior to Manassas, as I later realized, I had placed too many burdens on Marjie and my family. Through the sometimes-trying times at Manassas, I learned the value of pastoral peer groups, with whom I could share my deepest feelings. I value such mutual support among pastoral friends.

Also regular exercise helped me. Strenuous and enjoyable activities such as handball, racquetball, jogging, and swimming worked wonders in my life. Even yard work was a good release, although I do admit to relishing it less than racquetball.

A Long Process

A while back I showed a written account of those first years to one member and asked for comments. The member said, "Your strategies, conscious or not, worked, but the healing process took far longer than any of us would have thought." The key words are *worked* and *took far longer*.

That my strategies *worked* doesn't mean they were perfect. Some problems continued during my years in Manassas, and when I retired, work yet remained to be done. Many dedicated members did too much and burned out. At times, some members had an Elijah complex: "I alone am left." I know I hurt some members — unintentionally — but still they were hurt. Some members left the church because they felt they couldn't work with me.

But healing did take place, although not in the span of the three or four years I had envisioned. There were two important watersheds in the healing process, at ten and fifteen years after my arrival at Manassas.

It was in the tenth year that the man who had accosted me while I was jogging joined the church. He immediately became active in worship, Bible study, and service. Also at the ten-year mark, the church planned a celebration for Marjie's ministry as well as mine. Not only did we enjoy it, but it indicated that the leadership could take initiative again, and that they believed there was something to celebrate.

I retired fifteen years after going to Manassas, announcing it several months before it happened. The members' response was a marvel to behold. The leaders formed committees to plan our retirement festivities and to work toward finding interim and continuing pastoral leadership. The church members accepted tasks and provided feedback on what they considered to be the needs of the church. In all, the church spirit was reminiscent of the words of the apostle Paul: "The one thing I do is to forget what is behind me and do my best to reach what is ahead."

Certainly the transition into a church torn by a difficult experience with a previous pastor is not the easiest. But my experience at Manassas Baptist helped me understand Paul's statement: "I have worked harder than anyone else. It wasn't I; it was the grace of God."

PART FOUR

Shaping the Future

Congregations and pastors may not argue about where to squeeze the toothpaste tube, but after the honeymoon, they have inevitable conflicts that need to be resolved.

— *Doug Scott*

CHAPTER ELEVEN

After the Honeymoon

My wife and I had been separated by 3,000 miles of ocean for five years before our wedding. Our fragile relationship had been sustained by letters, cassettes, and occasional transatlantic telephone calls. When I finally arrived at her home in England for two weeks of frantic wedding and honeymoon planning, we felt frightened and pressured.

Fragile relationship, frantic planning — that's not unlike the beginning of a new pastorate. So, like couples, congregations look forward to the honeymoon. After the anxiety and excitement of calling a new pastor, they long to settle into an unhurried time where pastor and congregation can get to know one another.

But then what? After the first year, sometimes the first month, couples have to hammer out a working relationship; they must resolve the myriad of conflicts that arise in the normal course of marriage.

Congregations and pastors may not argue about where to squeeze the toothpaste tube, but after the honeymoon, they too have inevitable conflicts that need to be resolved.

In particular, I have encountered at least five areas that have confronted me and my congregations after the honeymoon.

Caring for Yourself

Some issues in congregational life everyone cares about — the appearance of the sanctuary, the stability of the budget, the Sunday school program. But some issues no one cares about — at least almost no one. People don't care whether the newsletter is printed on long or short grain paper; they don't care what kind of floor cleaner is used. And hard as it is to admit, many don't care whether their pastor works too hard, or whether their pastor has spent time with his or her family.

Like many other clergy, I entered parish ministry assuming that as long as I gave my all to my church, the people would take care of my family and me. I have since learned that such an assumption is not only untrue, it is also unfair to my congregation.

My revelation was not only abrupt, it was also embarrassing. I was in my first senior pastorate, facing a long agenda, and I had few resources. My congregation was pleasant, friendly, and dedicated to a pace that, in my youth and inexperience, I found maddeningly slow. So, in order to compensate for their inaction, I doubled my level of activity, setting an example (I thought) for them to follow.

After a few months, my anxiety increased as they accepted my frenzied level of work but resolutely maintained their own. One evening, I came to a vestry meeting not having spent a night home in weeks, and during the rector's report, I lost it.

"I am beginning to feel frustrated," I said as patiently as I could. "I am doing a tremendous amount of work around here with little or no response. I've increased the number of programs available to the congregation; I'm visiting and going to meetings; plus I'm preparing sermons and classes. I see our shut-ins every week and go to the hospital every day. I'm not looking for praise (although I probably was), but I feel that my commitment isn't being matched by the leadership of this parish!" There was a long silence, where I felt people were doing some serious self-examination.

Finally, one wise and patient vestry member, who had seen rectors come and go, quietly said, "I expect you, as my pastor, to take care of yourself. I think that's a big part, perhaps the biggest part, of your job. A burned-out priest is of no use to me or to my church. Not one person here can take care of you or set reasonable limits for you. We look to you for leadership in the management of your life. I'm no theologian, but from Scripture and from your preaching about the kingdom of God, I've learned that it is our responsibility to be stewards of that kingdom, to manage what we have, including our time and work, in a mature and responsible way. That's what we brought you here to do."

I have blessed that man a thousand times in my prayers and have tried to implement his charge throughout my ministry. After the honeymoon we're tempted to begin making the many necessary changes, to plunge into the work of the church now that we've built trust. But in the process we're tempted to abuse ourselves and our families. That's when we fail our congregations and the Lord who calls us to wholeness. As simple as it sounds, only I am in charge of me. In exercising self-care, I exercise Christ's ministry.

Beyond Fighting or Dying

A few years ago, I received a call from a prominent member who wanted to talk to me about the direction the church was heading. He said he wanted to bring along a number of my "good friends" — a sure sign of trouble. The meeting time arrived, a cold November afternoon, and for four hours I sat and listened to my "good friends" tell me everything they thought was wrong with me and my ministry: My attitude was wrong; my personality wasn't what the church needed; I offended and upset people; I was too pushy when it came to the design and implementation of programs; my administrative skills were weak; I lacked warmth and wasn't approachable.

Of course, they said, everyone agreed that I was a great preacher, but that alone wasn't enough. My only recourse, as they saw it, was to leave the church before I did any more damage. It hurt them to say it, but perhaps I really ought to consider leaving the ministry, seeking an occupation that was more in line with my ministry, becoming a trial lawyer, for instance.

Sitting across from my "friends," my heart in my mouth, my face red, my hands trembling, I knew what Pogo meant when he said, "We have met the enemy and he is us." Having listened to other clergy who have faced this kind of aggressive assault, I've noticed that we respond to such hostility in one of two ways. We either fight or die.

My first urge is to try to correct misinformation or misperceptions. This is a strong and seductive yearning. "This isn't true," "You don't understand," or "Let me explain" want to spill out. But combatants usually don't care about facts. Their anger and frustration are not based on data but on some dark pain that I, their target, cannot touch with facts.

Consequently, if we fight back, trying to convince or persuade, we simply make things worse, convincing our assailants we are entrenched in our stubbornness or self-delusion. "You see," they say, "we tried to tell him, but he just wouldn't listen."

At one point in my conversation with these people, one of the participants said to me, "I wonder if you could list the families in this church who like you?" List them? I could provide a computer printout! But would it convince my angry friend? Not likely.

If we choose not to fight, though, we may elect to die. We may accept the whipping of angry folk, internalize the pain, and carry the burdened agenda of others. All too often we take the pain to another area of our life and hope to have it healed there, by burdening our family with our agony or letting the anger and resentment slip into sermons or withdrawing from our people.

In the end, the stress eats away at our bodies and our souls until one or the other is consumed, or we turn bitter.

I have found, however, that there is a solution beyond fighting or dying, a way that owes much to the work of Rabbi Edwin Friedman and his landmark book, *Generation to Generation: Family Process in Church and Synagogue* (Guilford Press, 1985). The process involves two steps: gathering information and telling the truth.

One of the first things I did after the encounter with my hostile friends was to look carefully at the history of my parish. I read through vestry minutes, gathered oral history, and wrote down the pattern of clergy-laity conflict in the congregation. I found, much to my surprise and relief, that there was a long history of personal confrontation with the clergy of the church, with significant numbers of people moving in and out of the church because of their conflicts with the rector. It helped to know that this wasn't something new, and that the other clergy here had faced the same thing at regular intervals.

Second, I took the calculated risk of telling other people in the congregation the truth about what had happened to me. I didn't try to make the story more palatable. I didn't try to protect others or myself by concealing information or the identity of the participants. In telling the story, I did not try to convince or coerce but rather tried to get accurate information in response.

Friedman insists that secrets feed corporate illness, allowing the problem to continue. The phrase, "Everybody says . . ." is destructive because everybody can be somebody or nobody; in either case it can't be confronted effectively unless brought out in the open.

Thus, when my wife and I would have members of the congregation to dinner, or when I would visit in members' homes, I would say something like, "You know, a few weeks ago, Bob, Bill, John, and Harry came to see me, and here's what they said. . . . Do you think their analysis is accurate? What do you think about their conclusions? I would really like to know how you feel about what they said."

At the beginning of the process, I was nervous about sharing this incident with members of the church, afraid that my "friends" were close to being right, and even more afraid of admitting my failure to keep peace in the church. But this approach had four positive results.

First, it provided me with concrete data about the topics raised in the conflict. Second, it elicited support and encouragement from members of the congregation. Third, it allowed the people I asked to own the issues themselves; so I honored them and their views in the asking. Fourth, it gave me specifics for use in subsequent discussions with those who confronted me.

I then returned to the critical group and said honestly, "I listened to you carefully and took what you said seriously. Since we met, I have spoken to fifty-some people, sharing with them the things you said to me. I have found that most people here aren't, in fact, concerned about those things you were worried about. I am sure that must come as a real relief to you." With that, the attack of this group ended.

I'll never choose to fight or die again.

Getting Sea Legs

When I was a boy, my father and I were invited to go deep-sea fishing on a friend's boat. As the boat pitched and rolled through the waves, I was thrown back and forth across the deck until my father stood next to me and showed me how to plant my feet, bend my legs, and shift my weight from side to side so the waves wouldn't throw me around.

We all face waves in parish ministry, especially once the novelty of our new pastorate wears off or the congregation's tolerance of our newness or insufficiency lessens. The waves may be seasonal like the high pitch of Christmas or the low basin of summer worship. They may be political as a board faces financial crisis or months of ordinary inactivity. A series of pastoral crises drain us of energy or periods of counseling calm may threaten to take the edge off our skills.

"I can't stand Christmas," an ordained friend once complained. "Every year I go nonstop from Thanksgiving through Christmas, and by the time Christmas Eve services arrive, I feel drained and have nothing to say."

"I haven't spoken to my wife in a month," another complained. "We've been planning for our capital campaign, and the details have been overwhelming. When I do get home, which isn't often enough, I can't begin to explain it all, so I don't say anything. I turn on the television set just to give me an excuse not to talk."

I was hit by a particularly large wave myself not long ago: our Parish House, the education wing of our church, burned down. In the weeks and months that followed, I was overwhelmed by the details that were necessary to settle insurance, assess damage, reschedule space and programs, plan a new building, and hire a contractor. Consequently, I ignored my family and my own needs for recreation and growth — knocked over again.

The development of spiritual sea legs that enable us to ride out the waves of ministry depend on a few things.

First, we must recognize that waves are part of the seascape. "When are the problems going to end?" an ordained friend recently complained to me. "I never seem to get to the place where the church is stable or quiet. It's just one problem after another. I've got money problems at church and at home. I don't have enough time for my children or my wife, let alone myself. I've been hanging on, waiting for a break, but I don't think one is coming."

My friend viewed problems as an extraordinary part of the scenario. My own experience is that parish ministry is a daily exercise of problem solving on a number of different levels, from the absurd to the vital. In fact, recently in re-reading the Gospel of Mark, I noticed that Jesus is in trouble throughout the account. An accurate view of what we do helps us see that waves will just keep coming, so we better adapt.

Developing sea legs, however, also means having our feet planted in at least two different spots. The individual planted in only one place is bound to lose balance in even the calmest water.

I suspect that many of us find that we are planted in the place where we work and the place where we live. While there is always some crossover of interest in a clergy home, our health will depend largely on our ability to keep those two places separate from one another, so that home and office are distinct. If office and home is each oriented toward work, one cannot provide respite when the other throws us off balance.

But we can increase our balance by putting down other legs as well — by continuing our education, or meeting with a group of colleagues, or practicing an avocation. One friend, an active volunteer in an AIDS center, finds his balance in a trout stream in the Catskill Mountains. I find my balance through the lens of a camera.

But sea legs don't help unless I know when to shift my weight. For instance, I've learned to shift my weight to my family before Easter season, investing my time in my wife and children, seeking the presence of the risen Lord in my home. Then, when the demands of the Easter season come, I am prepared to give myself to the church.

Managing Malaise

A few years ago, I was caught in discouragement. I felt I was getting nowhere with my congregation. We had hit a slump together, and I didn't see hope for much progress. Worse, I began to feel my skills were underused and that my job had become lifeless.

A telephone call from the search committee of a large congregation in northern California sparked my interest. The parish self-study arrived in the mail, and it seemed at last that a congregation that wanted my kind of ministry had come knocking at my door. My wife and I threw ourselves into prayer and study about the possibility of this call. When I was asked to come to California for a week of interviews and orientation, we were galvanized with excitement. We had our eyes firmly fixed on the prize ahead and arranged to take some vacation time to accept the interview.

Unfortunately, I ignored the congregation where I had been called to serve. By the time the search committee voted for their choice, we had invested three months of anticipation and excitement into the new job. We were convinced our future was in this new congregation. The congregation wasn't. The committee, in a close vote, called someone else. Our excitement and hopes were dashed, our spirits as low as they could be, and we had so emotionally disengaged from our home that returning was a bitter disappointment.

In the meantime, someone from our church got wind we were interviewing elsewhere, despite our earnest attempts to keep it quiet. News of our planned departure spread through the congregation like wildfire, and within a matter of days, we were faced by an angry parish. People had no difficulty telling us how they felt, and one person in particular bluntly stated the feelings of many: "You've spent all this time telling us how we were a family in Christ, and then you do something like this behind our backs. It's like having one of your parents file for divorce without telling you they were unhappy."

When I tried to explain the emotional state that led me to accept the interview, he said, "We all felt like we were in a rut, but you didn't see any of us running off to a different church. We expected that you would stick it out with us."

Naturally, there are plenty of times when we can legitimately look for another church. The question here is not how we manage our careers, but rather how we manage our malaise. In looking back on that time, I see that I might have found a way to share my feelings about our common life. I could have looked to the congregation for energy, engaging them to help instead of going outside my own community of faith. I've also discovered that talking about a contemplated move with church leadership is not always suicidal.

My predecessor in one church talked openly about his uncertainty about staying before he finally moved a year later. While the members of the church found his struggle unsettling and painful, they also valued his openness and his willingness to expose himself to criticism. His honesty made the decision, when it finally came, a conclusion to a congregational time of waiting and prayer, whether or not that decision was welcomed.

When my own vision is clouded, I've learned to seek clarity from the people I serve, and to present myself to them for their ministration instead of drawing apart. This is a difficult way to respond to malaise, for both congregation and pastor, and it must be handled with great tact. But it can also be a valuable service to all.

Waiting Together

Inevitably, pastors face personal crises — our marriage becomes strained, finances burden us, our children's behavior or poor health trouble us. When that happens, how do we respond? In particular, how much do we tell the congregation?

On the one hand, we are called to be authentic with our people. We don't want to put on an act, as if the Christian life for us is victory unto victory. On the other hand, pastoral crises, when they become known, can occupy the life and mind of a congregation to an extraordinary degree, detracting people from the work of the church and devotion to our Lord.

Over the years I have asked ordained friends how they handle such moments. "I put on my smiling face as I go out the door," said one, "and take it off again when I come home. What happens in my house is none of their business."

Another friend said, "How can I involve them in my problems? As soon as I step out of my role, it's very difficult to get back in it again. I may share some information with them, but I can't disrupt the basic nature of our relationship."

Still another found it difficult to handle the response of individuals with whom he shared such crises. "I remember trying to impress on one man the difficulty I was having living within the restrictions of my salary. He pulled out a checkbook and wrote me a check for one hundred dollars. I felt cheap and small. I beat myself all the way home for trying to share a problem with him."

I became acutely aware of this tension when my third daughter was born seven weeks premature. At the time, her doctors were not sure about her chances for complete health. It was the greatest crisis my wife and I had faced.

In the few days between her birth and Sunday services, we struggled with how to present our situation to the congregation. We needed to have their prayers and would welcome their care, but we also needed some space and were afraid my wife would be bombarded with visitors and the refrigerator stuffed with unwanted tuna casseroles. We knew they would be anxious to help, but we were afraid the help would be more than we could stand. We shared the problem with the hospital chaplain, who happened to be a good friend.

"Tell them what has happened," he said. "Then tell them what you need. Tell them how to help, and tell them what to do. But most of all, tell them to wait with you."

Dutch theologian Henri Nouwen has written beautifully about the process of waiting, drawing our attention to the story of Elizabeth and Mary. As soon as Mary knew that she and Elizabeth had both conceived, she went to her cousin to wait for God's story to unfold.

That Sunday, I asked our friends to wait with us. In the weeks ahead, I shared our daughter's progress with them, not as news to which they were entitled, but as events that we waited for together in patience and prayer. Thankfully, the day arrived when I could assure them that our wait was at an end and that Joy, our daughter, had regained full health. Our ordeal had become not a distraction, but a part of their journey in faith.

If the honeymoon is a time when pastor and congregation get to know one another, after the honeymoon is a time when pastor and congregation figure out how to live together. That means learning to handle — with honesty, patience, and understanding — the many and inevitable ups and downs of parish life.

Saying good-by properly is one thing. Starting a new life is another. But both are part of preparing for retirement.
— *Ed Bratcher*

CHAPTER TWELVE

Preparing for Retirement

Retirement is a good-news/bad-news story. The good news is that retirement provides time to do many things we have had to put off through life. In this sense, retirement is a life-giving experience. The bad news is that much of life as we've known it is lost. In this sense, retirement is a deathlike experience.

And sometimes it feels like both simultaneously. Upon my retirement, a friend wrote about his of two years: "As I look back, I must say that the relocation, the complete change of lifestyle, and the economic adjustments have been dramatic, and these changes

continue at a pace that keeps me constantly running to catch-up."
My friend's advice to me? "Good luck!"

Jesting aside, I believe we can do better (and my friend would
agree). In fact, the better we prepare for retirement, the more we'll
experience resurrection through the grief of retirement and joy in
the new life retirement brings. In particular, I found it helpful to
prepare in two distinct ways: I had to prepare to leave and prepare
to live.

Preparing to Leave

Before I can begin retirement, I have to retire. That means
leaving a church family I've grown to love. Preparing to leave, then,
means preparing the church for my departure and saying a proper
good-by. I found a variety of tasks to attend to before leaving.

• *Give the church good warning.* I officially announced my
retirement seven months in advance, but I had informed our board
of deacons five months prior to that.

I found a year's notice to the church leaders to be about right.
The deacons then had time to prepare themselves and the church
for my departure. And the seven months notice to the congregation
gave my wife, Marjie, and me time to say good-by yet without
dragging it out.

• *Let the board lead.* I felt the board was primarily responsible
for preparing the church for my departure. I could give guidance
and encouragement, but the board needed to take initiative. They
needed to outline steps that would be taken, and they had to keep
the congregation informed. Soon I wouldn't be around, and they'd
have to fend for themselves while searching for a new pastor. Better
to let them get their wings while I was around.

Fortunately, our deacons didn't hesitate to assume this leadership. By the time of my public announcement, they were ready to
appoint from their group a Pastoral Transition Committee. After a
few weeks of study this committee then recommended the congregation form three committees: the Bratcher Celebration Committee,
the Interim Pastor Search Committee, and the Pastor Search
Committee.

The board was on its way.

● *Give guidance to the board.* Even though the board must take leadership during the transition, I gave guidance to the board and the committees it had established. I offered suggestions about what to read, what to do next, and who to contact for further advice.

One book I recommended they read was Roy Oswald's *Running Through the Thistles: Terminating a Ministerial Relationship* (Alban Institute). I gave my copy to the Pastoral Transition Committee, and the committee took its recommendations to heart, including my margin notes and underlining! This made the retirement procedure a tailor-made process for Marjie and me.

Yet after getting things started, I felt it best to adopt a hands-off policy. I tried to show I had complete confidence in the board and congregation.

● *Remember the congregation.* The board should be particularly sensitive to the congregation during the transition. And the depth of the congregation's anxiety depends in part on the length of the retiring pastor's term.

For example, at Manassas we soon realized that 60 percent of the congregation had joined the church during my pastorate. That meant the majority of the members could not remember the previous pastoral change. As a whole, these members were more anxious and needed greater reassurance as to what to expect.

In light of this, the Pastoral Transition Committee held two "listening sessions." At these Wednesday evening two-hour sessions, the committee explained what they were doing and why; then they listened to the questions, suggestions, and concerns of the members.

Not that all suggestions were automatically enacted by the committee. For example, some members felt that the only task was finding a new pastor, and that this should have been started yesterday! The committee believed, however, that a period of "grief" was in order, that the church should unhurriedly say good-by to me before they devoted themselves fully to finding a new pastor. They explained this to the congregation and then proceeded in light of it.

● *Protect the staff.* The retirement of the senior minister also puts pressure on the church staff. Many church members assume that if there are two or three full-time associates, they will take over the duties of the senior minister (with the possible exception of preaching). This assumption implies that the other duties of the associates are relatively unimportant.

The staff, however, can become resentful about having to sacrifice some of their responsibilities. In addition, they are concerned about their future, wondering about their ability to work with the future senior pastor, or simply the security of their jobs.

The concern about job security I had tried to settle earlier. During the last five years of my ministry, the Manassas church called two associates. In each case, I spoke to the personnel committee about these calls beforehand. I recommended, and the committee agreed, that these ministers be called by the congregation, and that their positions be in the hands of the church, not the present or future senior minister.

(If that hadn't been the case, I would have spoken about my retirement to my staff well in advance of the board. I would have worked closely with the board and the staff to insure that their needs, especially for relocation, were given priority.)

In addition, the chair of the Pastoral Transition Committee invited the staff to meet with the committee regularly. There the staff could discuss the transition from their perspective, airing any grievances they had.

• *Don't call attention to yourself.* I have seen congregations become anxious when the retiring pastor started marking the end of his ministry with remarks like, "This is my last Thanksgiving service" and two weeks later "This is my last Communion service" and so on.

Besides creating undue grief, this seems like a form of exhibitionism. It draws too much attention to the pastor. I feel that, especially when I'm leading worship, no matter the circumstance, the attention should be on God. So even my last Christmas Eve Communion service, a moving service held a week before my retirement, I celebrated as we had year by year.

• *Visit the particularly needy.* Before I retired, I tried to make calls on two types of people: the home bound and those with whom I had strained relationships. I felt the home bound needed to be reassured they were not forgotten. And I wanted to make every effort to settle disagreements with those from whom I was estranged — for their spiritual welfare and mine.

For example, I visited one family who had not been active for about five years. They were not comfortable with some of my views and had been attending other churches (although they maintained their membership at Manassas). After exchanging pleasantries, I acknowledged our differences, mentioned my respect for their views, and asked if we couldn't at least part with a measure of graciousness. I am happy to say they accepted the invitation and have since renewed their ties to the church.

● *Work like a healthy duck.* Conventional wisdom has it that when pastors announce their retirement, they immediately become lame ducks. On the contrary, I felt that if I didn't act like a lame duck, I would not be treated as such.

In administration and long-range planning, of course, my leadership style had to change. If I wasn't going to be around to experience the effects of decisions, I didn't think I should participate in making them.

For example, the church at Manassas was well into a building program when I announced my retirement. While the building committee continued its work, made presentations to the congregation, took votes, and put out plans for bids, I was nowhere to be seen. My absence from these business meetings was a way of saying that I had confidence in their ability to move ahead without me.

Besides, I had more than enough to do. In fact, during my last seven months I couldn't get it all done. Each day was full of opportunities, frustrations, victories, and defeats — like every other day of my ministry. Preaching became a time to focus on the great themes of the gospel. Evangelism and outreach took on an even greater urgency for me. And counseling became a process of making appropriate referrals before leaving — no small task.

And on my last Sunday, I preached, conducted a baptismal service, received new members into the church, and said my good-bys to a fifteen-year pastorate.

Frankly, I didn't have time to be a lame duck!

● *Say good-by well.* Based on my reading of Roy Oswald's pamphlet, I felt that my good-by should be a time of celebration — celebration of the good things that had taken place between the people and me.

The deacon committee at Manassas Baptist agreed and appointed a subcommittee to accomplish this end — the Bratcher Celebration Committee. Their goal was to celebrate my fifteen-year pastorate at Manassas as well as the forty-two years of ministry Marjie and I enjoyed.

The celebration was built around three services. The first was held on a Sunday evening, which happened to be my birthday. We enjoyed a time of worship built around my favorite anthems and hymns, and then we followed with a reception.

The second celebration was held on the Sunday before Marjie's birthday. That service, held at the conclusion of morning worship, focused on thanksgiving for Marjie's ministry. A reception also followed.

The third celebration was a retirement banquet held after morning worship three weeks before I retired. There were several brief speeches by members of my family, church members, ministerial colleagues, and denominational executives. A special surprise was the main speaker — an Episcopal priest who for many years had been my closest colleague in Manassas. Although he had since moved from Virginia to Florida, the committee had paid his expenses to bring him back!

Gifts and mementos were presented, including a book of letters and an album of photographs. Included were photographs taken, table by table, of all 350-plus people present at the banquet.

● *Prepare your spouse.* In some ways, retirement can be more traumatic for the spouse than for the retiree. Furthermore, I didn't want Marjie to simply tag along at my retirement festivities.

So I encouraged the celebration committee, upon the advice of a friend, to have that special celebration for her. I called friends in each of the churches we had served and asked them to write letters expressing appreciation for Marjie's unique contributions to our ministry. Portions of these letters were read at her celebration service.

In addition, we spent many hours in deep conversation, sharing our feelings, hopes, dreams, and fears about retirement. We knew that retirement would be a challenge and that we needed each other's support.

Preparing to Live

Saying good-by properly is one thing. Starting a new life is another. But both are part of preparing for retirement. To help us set out on our new life, we did advance preparation in at least five areas.

• *Moving.* I feel that a pastor should move away from the church's community upon retirement. The pastor and congregation need to make a complete break with each other. Otherwise the next pastor will have to deal both with the memory *and* the physical presence of the former pastor — and one is hard enough.

Sometimes, of course, it's not possible to move, at least immediately — if, for instance, the church gives the pastor and spouse the parsonage as a retirement present. In such cases, pastors must set clear guidelines about their future relationship with the church and its new pastor. Even then, the retired pastor might consider moving after two or three years.

Any move is difficult; it's not only expensive but draining to make new friends, get established with doctors and dentists, change addresses, and so on. But I think moving after retirement is more difficult still. In previous moves, the pastor and family always had a host of new friends waiting for them, ready to help them settle in. Upon retirement, however, that is usually not the case.

Finances can also constrain the retirement move. The pastor feels a pressure to make the right choice of home and community, because few retired pastors can afford the luxury of moving a second time.

Consequently, Marjie and I started talking seriously about our move eighteen months before retirement. We purchased books on retirement communities where we might live. The books listed the cost of housing, medical facilities, cultural opportunities, recreational activities, and climate. We then listed our priorities and started the process of looking. Our final decision, however, was not made until the first month after retirement.

• *Finances.* Financial preparation for retirement is a life-long endeavor. Most denominations offer or require their pastors to be enrolled in a retirement program, in addition to social security. The equity of one's home also works toward retirement.

Some pastors have to use parsonages and consequently can't build any equity. But even that drawback can be worked with, especially if such pastors recognize the problem early and make wise investments in other areas.

Owning one's home does not solve every problem, of course. It's important, for example, to allow sufficient time to sell it. It took us nine months to sell ours. To help the church go about the task of calling a new pastor, we made arrangements to move three months after retirement. That gave us peace of mind, but paying for two homes for a time was difficult.

In terms of saving for retirement, we finally made our major push for retirement when I was about 50. At that point we had paid the bulk of our children's educational expenses. We secured advice from denominational retirement planners and tax accountants on how to increase our savings programs. We had to cut back on our standard of living, but the sacrifices have paid nice benefits in peace of mind after retirement.

We wanted to enter retirement with a fairly new car — and paid for. So three to four years before retirement we began planning for the automobile we would need.

Immediately prior to retirement, we tried to plan for the first six months of retirement — months when expenses are heavy. For a change, *we* had to pay moving expenses, and they weren't tax deductible. Furthermore, I found it was unrealistic to expect extra income from pulpit supplies and interim pastorates during this period.

All in all, we enjoyed many happy moments during the first six months of retirement, in spite of the changes in lifestyle. I am glad we had the financial resources to make those months relatively worry free.

● *Activities.* Marjie and I also found it helpful to plan what we would be doing with ourselves for the first couple of years of retirement.

For example, two of my goals were to research and write on the personal and professional needs of ministers. So I wanted to be near a good seminary library. Two or three years after retirement I wanted to start supplying pulpits and interim pastorates.

I also want to enjoy some fun activities in retirement. Unfortunately my two mainstays in this area — traveling and racquetball — are not as easy to pursue as I had hoped. I am finding that the high cost of traveling and my irregular schedule get in the way of those pursuits. So I am in the process of trying to develop other interests, such as reading fiction.

● *Continuing ministry.* I also have tried to prepare myself for continuing my ministry. First, I set clear guidelines about under what circumstances I would return to my last pastorate for weddings and funerals. Second, I found a new church home.

Frankly, I've found it hard to adjust to being a nonstaff church member. But I've made every effort to attend not only worship but business meetings, fellowship gatherings, and Sunday school classes. At these meetings I keep my opinions to myself, unless specifically asked, and even then I try to speak only a helpful word.

In addition, I'm willing to serve in these areas but only at the request of the congregation or pastor. I also try to do these things as a church member, not as a former pastor, and I avoid saying or implying, "This is the way I did it when I was pastor."

● *The first month.* One of the areas in which Marjie and I had completely different views was on what to do the first month. My inclination was to plan nothing. While the months before retirement had been unusually happy, they were also extremely busy. I saw the first month, therefore, as a time to relax.

Marjie, on the other hand, felt we needed to leave town the

first day and be gone for at least a month. Her rationale was that for both the church and us (more particularly for me) there needed to be a physical separation. That was the only way the reality of retirement would sink in. I finally agreed to go along with her preference.

So we planned a couple of trips that first month. But during the first two weeks of travel, I received three phone calls from the church office! Even my absence was not enough to make the break complete.

The fact is, one of the church members died, and people thought I should know. But the family finally decided — partly because I was away — to have the associate pastors officiate at the memorial service. That decision helped me and the members of the church begin accepting the idea that I had indeed retired.

Marjie was right.

Six months into retirement I called a friend, also recently retired, and invited him and his wife to have lunch with Marjie and me. He asked, "What day will be convenient?"

I replied, "Any day but Wednesday."

He laughed and said, "It's quite a change to have a choice, isn't it?"

It is. And the more planning we do before retirement, the more choices we'll have in retirement.

Transitions, in the final analysis, are the couplings between the cars of ministry. The engine may pull the cars, and the cars may carry the freight, but only if everything is firmly coupled.

— *James D. Berkley*

Epilogue

When our few-dozen years of active ministry are finished, and we're enjoying a rousing game of golf with our old seminary buddies from the retired-pastors home, what would we want to be said about our ministries? How would we like people to remember us?

- "He loved the Lord and his people." Yes, I'd like that.
- "When she preached, we heard God's Word!" How nice!
- "He was a pastors' pastor." Touching.
- "He moved well." Well — no. Not exactly. It's great to

make sound decisions about calls, but our transitions ought hardly be our pinnacles of success.

"He moved well" sounds more fitting for a Michael Jordan or a Mikhail Baryshnikov. Such an accolade might even work for a Lee Iacocca, whose career move to Chrysler came up golden. But for a pastor? No.

Transitions, themselves, aren't ministry. But that doesn't classify them as unimportant. Our authors have clearly shown the opposite. Transitions, in the final analysis, are the couplings between the cars of ministry. The engine may pull the cars, which carry the freight, but only if everything is firmly coupled.

So we want to make wise transitions. We want to go where God, not our ambitions or desire for ease, lead us. We wouldn't mind finding that just-right pastorate in which we utterly thrive. The reason, however, is that when we make a good transition, we can minister that much more effectively.

And successful transitions, according to our authors, are a matter of attention to detail. Each one in his own way made that point. This is not a time to take things for granted, but to pray diligently and plan carefully.

So we hope you've gained some mastery over pastoral transitions through reading this book. And we pray that those transitions —timely and well-executed — will lead you into long and productive pastoral relationships that make transitions few and that point people toward the greatest transition of all: into glory.